Preface

I have been involved with English language testing since 1960. During that time I have scored, developed, written, constructed, pretested, and evaluated English as a Second Language (ESL) tests. Many who speak English as a second language have been my friends and colleagues as well as my students.

Many students of English are required to show that they can perform successfully as students in such fields as architecture, business, engineering, medicine, music, social work, etc. However, they are not sure of the proficiency level they should have reached in English to do this. Also, they are not sure what will be on the English test they are required to take.

These students wonder about the content of the Michigan English Language Assessment Battery (MELAB) test. They ask how to prepare for it. They are worried, and obviously what they need is a sample test to show them the format and difficulty level of the actual test, so that they can evaluate themselves.

Some of these students are proficient in English and should not worry about their performance on the test. They do not need more English instruction or practice, but they do need a self-assessment test and a model test to give them an idea of the content, the level of difficulty, and the testing method used in the MELAB. On the other hand, some students may have weaknesses of which they are not aware. They also need self–assessment so they can work to improve performance on their weak areas.

It is for all these students that I have written this book. I, and other test writers, want students to perform at their optimum—that is, do the best they can do—on our tests. We do not want students to get low scores just because they are not familiar with the test format or directions or have difficulty timing themselves. We hope students will familiarize themselves with these processes so that they can do their best. We don't want students to be afraid of the test. We want them to be familiar with its content and format and to be prepared.

This test book is not, therefore, designed to be memorized but to be studied as an approach to a certain kind of task or testing method. The best way to prepare for any test is to be competent (skilled and knowledgable) in the *subject matter*. The best way to study for the MELAB, or any other English language test, is to study English, rather than to study or memorize a test preparation book. Memorizing the sample tests in this book will not guarantee success on the MELAB or any other ESL test; studying and using English for reading, writing, listening, and speaking, over a long period of time, is the best way to become an expert user of English.

I wish to thank those who so generously supported me in this project: Sue Reinhart, who helped with the grammar commentaries; Joan Morley, who advised me on the listening portions, and her students, who critiqued the listening test; the two anonymous reviewers, for their insightful and substantive comments and suggestions on the preliminary manuscript; and my colleague Sarah Briggs and my husband David, who provided motivation and support.

A Student's Guide to the MELAB

Mary C. Spaan

Ann Arbor

THE UNIVERSITY OF MICHIGAN PRESS

Copyright © by the University of Michigan 1992, 2007
All rights reserved
ISBN 10: 0-472-03254-2
ISBN 13: 978-0-472-03254-9
Published in the United States of America by
The University of Michigan Press
Manufactured in the United States of America
⊗ Printed on acid-free paper

2010   2009   2008   2007   4 3 2 1

Contents

Introduction

What is the MELAB?

The English Language Institute at the University of Michigan (ELI-UM) has made its English language proficiency testing services available to institutions of higher education (universities) as well as to businesses and government agencies for over thirty years. The ELI-UM oversees the administration of the Michigan English Language Assessment Battery (MELAB), an advanced level English language proficiency test designed to measure the English language ability of adult nonnative speakers of English who will need to use the language for academic purposes at the university level. The MELAB has also been used for screening job training and fellowship applicants.

The official MELAB is a secure test. This means the actual tests are not for sale, but they may be administered through the ELI-UM's testing service. Official MELAB tests are arranged through the ELI-UM and administered by official MELAB examiners throughout the world. The examiners send test papers back to ELI-UM for scoring and reporting of scores.

The official MELAB consists of three parts; subscores on these components (parts) are averaged to produce the final score. These are scaled scores, not a number of correct responses to questions, and not a percentage score. (Scoring is explained further in Scoring and Interpreting Your Test.) The components of the MELAB are:

Part 1: Composition, a thirty-minute impromptu essay;
Part 2: Listening, a tape-recorded multiple-choice test measuring comprehension of spoken English; and
Part 3: Grammar, Cloze, Vocabulary, Reading, an objective multiple-choice test containing grammar, cloze reading, and vocabulary problems, and reading passages followed by comprehension questions.

An optional fourth part of the MELAB is an oral interview with the local examiner, who rates the candidate's spoken English. The oral interview is given to candidates for fellowships, grants, or job-training programs for GM (General Motors Corporation), the IMF (International Monetary Fund), UNDP (United Nations Development Programme), WHO (World Health Organization), and state nursing boards and is recommended for those candidates who wish to get financial assistance from a U.S. university in the form of a graduate student teaching assistantship. Any student applying to the University of Michigan should also have an oral interview.

What Is the Testing Procedure?

To receive a MELAB Information Bulletin, which contains a registration form, instructions, and sample test, you should contact:

> English Language Institute
> Testing and Certification
> The University of Michigan
> Ann Arbor, Michigan 48104
> Telephone: (734) 764-2461 / 866-696-3522, press 1
> Fax: (734) 615-6586
> Email: melabelium@umich.edu
> *www.lsa.umich.edu/eli/testing/melab*

To be eligible to take the test, you must not have taken the MELAB within the last six (6) weeks, and you must not have taken the MELAB more than four (4) times within a twelve (12)-month period.

If your test fees will not be paid by a sponsoring agency, you should send the English Language Institute a partial test fee when you send in your application form (the exact amount is given on the form and in ELI's instructions). The remainder of the test fee is paid to the examiner at the time of the test.

The ELI will send you the name and address of its MELAB examiner in your locality and will send the examiner authorization to test you. You should then contact the examiner and set a mutually convenient time for the test administration. The examiner conducts the test, which takes about two and one-half (2½) hours. The examiner sends all test papers to ELI for scoring and reporting. ELI will send score reports to you and to any institutions you have listed on your Identification Form.

The score report you receive will show your final MELAB score (this is the mathematical average of your separate scores for parts 1, 2, and 3), your separate part scores, and your oral rating, if you have taken the optional oral interview.

The entire procedure takes three to six weeks.

Official MELAB examiners are located in the cities listed in the MELAB Information Bulletin, which is available online and is regularly updated. New examiners can be added as needed. If there is no examiner in your area, you can tell this to the ELI Testing Office when you register for the MELAB and ask that someone be found to administer the test to you.

How To Use This Book

Students

This book will help you in the following ways:

1. The unknown is always a little frightening. By becoming familiar with the content and layout of the MELAB, you will gain confidence in your ability to do well on the test. Model tests, which you may take for practice, follow. Take plenty of time to look at the examples and read the instructions carefully before you begin each

practice test. This will help you to understand the test format and to practice some of the basics before you begin the practice test. The practice tests are not taken from the official MELAB. However, they were written and edited by the same people who write the MELAB. Some of the test items have appeared in other ELI tests.

2. You will get practice in following specific directions for taking this test. You should mark your answers to the practice test problems on one of the answer sheets in the appendix at the end of this book.

3. The MELAB will not only test your ability to use and recall written and spoken English, it will also test your fluency or speed in performing these tasks. The practice tests in this book will help you determine your speed. Before you begin a practice test, estimate how much quiet, uninterrupted time you will need to finish it, and then time yourself. (Take a watch or digital timer that does not beep with you to the actual MELAB if possible. Cell phones must be turned off.) Keep a record of how much time it took you to do each practice test. How much time did it take you? If it had been a real test, would you have finished within the time limit?

4. Farther back in the book there is a scoring key for each practice test. For the listening tests, there is a script and a commentary about what you heard on the tape recording. For the grammar, cloze, vocabulary, and reading practice tests, there is a commentary which explains the answers to the problems. You will be able to score your practice test and review your answers to the problems to see why the correct answer is correct.

5. After you score your practice test, you should go to the score interpretation section. You will be able to evaluate your performance on the test, to get some idea of how you might do on the official MELAB. You will see your strengths and weaknesses.

Reminder: The best way to prepare for any test is to know the subject thoroughly, not just to concentrate on the testing method. Just memorizing the sample tests in this book will not guarantee you success on the MELAB or any other English test. It takes years of study and practice to become highly proficient in a foreign language.

Teachers

The best way for students to prepare for the MELAB is to study and use a full range of English by reading widely, speaking with and listening to native speakers of English, and writing in English. They must practice English, not just memorize rules. Rules exist as helpful guidelines to explain why the language works the way it does.

It is important that this book be used as practice and familiarization for a certain kind of test, not as a "cram" book to be memorized. Memorization of this book will not by itself guarantee improved English language ability, nor will it guarantee improved performance on the MELAB. This book should not be used as the primary text for an ESL test preparation course. Rather, it should be considered supplemental to other textbooks that concentrate on the various skill areas to be measured. Appendix D lists suggested intermediate- and advanced-level texts for teaching the various skill areas.

If students have prepared well, they can be confident in their abilities, and they will not panic when it comes time to take a test. Taking a test is always a challenge; studying this book will ease the fear of the unknown for students taking the MELAB.

Test writers have a term called "task effect." This means that the test method may affect a student's performance on a test. Sometimes a proficient student will not do well on a test because s/he did not follow the directions or was unfamiliar with the test method and format. A test preparation book such as this one should eliminate negative task effect and produce an optimal and valid performance.

Most teachers prefer to work on one skill area at a time. Therefore, you might want to spend a week or two on each of the three mandatory parts of the MELAB.

Part 1. You might begin with timed impromptu essay writing. Begin by having your students write a timed thirty-minute essay on their choice of two topics given in this book or on other topics of your choosing. Then, review their essays.

1. Did they follow instructions? Did they write on only one of the topics? Did they write on both? Did the essay address the topic, or did it seem "off topic"?
2. Were they able to write at least 150–200 words?
3. Look at clarity and accuracy of expression and ability to develop a theme with supporting argument and details (examples). Is the meaning clear? Does the organization help make the thoughts clear and easy to follow? Are your students able to use complex as well as simple grammatical structures with a minimum of error? Do they use only simple sentence structures? Do they use a wide range of vocabulary appropriately? You may find it helpful to refer to the official MELAB composition descriptions and codes in appendix B.

You could have students repeat this process several times, getting feedback from you after each essay. Students can be trained to spend one or two minutes organizing their thoughts, and possibly writing an outline, twenty to twenty-five minutes writing, then three or four minutes reviewing what they have written and making corrections, additions, or other changes.

Part 2. Practice interactive speaking in class. Listen to both conversational dialogue and lecture tapes (both audio and video). Go over the examples and instructions for the listening test carefully. Then review:

1. Did they follow instructions? Did they mark their answers only on the answer sheets? Did they mark in the test booklets? Make sure they don't make mistakes in mechanics during the "real" test.
2. Were they able to keep up with the speed of the recording? Some students understand something the first time they hear it, others can understand if the aural stimuli is repeated, and still others have difficulty even with repetition.
3. Encourage them to make a guess if they aren't sure of what they heard. For the official test, they won't be able to review their responses and what they think they heard, but for these practice tests, you could have them write down what they thought they heard, and then discuss this when reviewing the correct answers.
4. Some students don't take any notes at all during the lecture and conversation parts of the listening test. Some of these just have very good aural memory and don't seem to need to take notes about details, while others don't understand what they

hear if it is in the form of longer discourse. Encourage your students to take notes, in outline form if possible, with some details. They should not write down *everything* they hear, but note only the important points or details. This practice will aid them not only on the MELAB, but also in university level coursework.

Check to see if errors occur more frequently in short utterance sections or in questions about longer discourse (the lecture and longer dialogue). Your students may need work on comprehending "fast speech," contractions, and idiomatic expressions. At lower proficiency levels, they may not be able to follow longer discourse (more than twenty seconds of continuous speech). At intermediate proficiency levels, they may understand the main idea of longer discourse but be unable to comprehend some of the details and how they relate to the main idea. Following scoring of your students' tests, the tape recording can be replayed as they read the script, so that the oral and written versions can be compared. You can help your students look for the main points of the lectures and conversations, as well as supporting details.

Part 3. For part 3, estimate percentages correct on each of the four sections. It may be that most of your students perform consistently on all sections of the test and just need general improvement and practice in all areas of the language. Others, however, may show relative strengths and weaknesses; for example, they may do well on reading but poorly on grammar, or vice versa. The commentaries following the answer keys can provide support for a review of the areas of weakness.

Before administering Practice Test 2, spend instructional time on each of the skill areas tested.

Practice Tests

Part 1: Composition

This is a 30-minute impromptu (unprepared) essay. You are not allowed to use a dictionary or other notes or aids while writing it. The examiner will give you a form with instructions and two topics on it. (See appendix A for a sample of this form.) You must write on *one* of the two topics. Do not try to write on both, and do not write about something else. If you write about something else, your paper will not be graded. If you do not understand the topics, ask the examiner to explain or translate them. Choose whichever topic is most interesting or appealing to you. Your choice will not make a difference in your score.

Make your topic choice quickly, then spend a minute or two planning your essay. If you wish, you may make an outline for your essay on the examination paper. You will not be graded on your outline; it is only to help you organize your thoughts. Once you begin writing, do not worry too much about minor errors you may have made; it is important that your writing be fluent (smooth-flowing) and not halting. When there are 5 minutes remaining, write a conclusion (ending or summary) to your essay. Then go back and edit it for additions, errors, or any other changes you wish to make. You may make these changes in the body of the essay, crossing out words and substituting others.

Do not waste time copying your composition over so that it looks nice; you will not be graded on the appearance of your paper. You will not be graded on penmanship (handwriting), but try to write legibly, so the graders can read it.

It will help you to practice writing 30-minute essays, both for general practice in writing and for practice in writing within this time limit. The essay topics might ask you to narrate an experience, to compare and contrast two things or ideas, to discuss the advantages and disadvantages of something, or possibly to take a position on a topic (have an opinion) and defend it (explain why you believe it, giving examples). Here are some examples of topics that have been used in the past:

1. What is the funniest thing that ever happened to you? Describe.
2. Would you raise your children the same way your parents raised you? Why or why not? Explain and give examples.
3. How should students be evaluated: according to their achievements or their effort? Discuss.
4. What do you think is the biggest environmental problem in your country? Explain in detail and tell what you think can be done to solve it.
5. What public figure, living or dead, do you admire most? Why?
6. What are the characteristics of a good teacher? Explain and give examples.
7. What are the problems of a student who wishes to study in a foreign country? Discuss university admissions, passport, visa, language problems, etc.

8. If you could give the President of the United States advice on improving relations with your country, what would you tell him?

9. Would you prefer to live in a large city or in the country (rural area)? Explain the reasons for your choice.

10. In your opinion, what are the causes of divorce? What do you think are the greatest problems caused by divorce?

11. For men: imagine that you were born a woman. How would your life be different? For women: imagine that you were born a man. How would your life be different? Explain and give examples.

12. If there were a country which was the single source of a major resource, would that country have the right not to share the resource with other countries? Why or why not?

13. If you could be another person for one day, who would you be, and how would you spend the time?

14. What advice would you give someone who wants to learn English?

15. Imagine that you are in charge of establishing the first colony on the moon. What kind of people would you choose to take with you? What qualities and technical skills should they have?

16. What are the effects of modern technology on the way of life in your country?

Remember, these are just examples of past topics, and they will *not* appear on your test. Do not try to memorize and write a composition on one of these topics when you take the MELAB.

All MELAB essays are graded at the English Language Institute at the University of Michigan. When assigning scores, the raters consider development of ideas or theme, organization and connection of ideas, fluency and clarity of expression, ability to use a variety of simple and complex syntactic structures, range and appropriateness of vocabulary, and ability to express things in detail and give good examples.

Compositions that contain only very short, simple sentences and simple vocabulary cannot be given the highest scores. If errors are not frequent and if they do not confuse your meaning, they will not lower your score much.

Each essay is read by at least two trained raters, who do not know each other's scores. If there is a great difference in the scores assigned the essay, a third rater will also score it. Reading is done holistically (a single overall score is given, rather than separate ratings for different things). Grades are assigned on a 10-point scale, with scores ranging from 97 to 53. Possible scores are 97, 93, 87, 83, 77, 73, 67, 63, 57, 53. If the graders assign two scores that are close to each other on the scale, an average score will be reported. For example, one score of 87 and the other of 83 will be reported as an 85. In addition, a letter code might be assigned. Letter codes show features of your writing that the graders thought were especially strong or weak in relation to the overall level of your writing. Appendix B lists the official MELAB composition numerical descriptions and letter codes.

Sample Essays

Here are some essays written by actual MELAB examinees. Before each essay, the score and a general description of what it represents are given. Following each essay is a discussion of the features that determined the raters' score.

Essay 1

Score 97. Very full, clear development of theme. Fluent, complex, broad vocabulary, error-free. Similar to well-educated adult native speaker of English who is also a good writer.

Topic: People who have been seriously injured can be kept alive by machines. Do you think they should be kept alive at great expense, or allowed to die?

1   There has been a lot of publicity recently about whether a person should be kept alive
2   by machines or allowed to die. This controversial question has generated a lot of
3   debate; on one hand, there are people who say that a person must be kept alive by
4   any means because no one has the right to decide whether a person should live or
5   die, while on the other hand, there are people who think that such a seriously injured
6   person should be allowed to die and not be kept dependent on a machine for the rest
7   of his or her life because allowing that person to die is more merciful.
8   Personally, I think that in certain cases where the patients are in great suffering
9   then it is more merciful to let the patient die in dignity. If there is no way that a
10   patient will ever recover and live independently of the machine then it would be kinder
11   to let the patient die. The Pro-Life group of people would argue that with so much
12   research going on there might one day be a cure for these patients and we shouldn't
13   allow them to die. Of course, such a cure might be found but could the patient's
14   relatives bear to see the suffering of the patient, living like a vegetable? I believe that
15   if the patient is in a sound mind and able to make his own decision then the patient
16   himself should be allowed to say whether he wants to live or die, otherwise it is his
17   close relative who should make the decision.
18   In cases where there is a very good chance that the patient will recover and does
19   not have to be dependent on the machine to be alive then it should be clear that he
20   be allowed to live. It can be also that the patient expresses a desire to live even though
21   heavily dependent on the machine; then of course, his wishes should be respected.
22   I think that it is a very sorry thing to keep hanging on to life attached to a machine
23   for the rest of one's life. After all, life is only worth living if one can live it with
24   dignity, to face each day with a challenge. Although I've never been in such a situation,
25   I can feel what it is like to be dependent on a machine for the rest of one's life. I
26   don't think the expense of keeping such a person alive should be the issue—the issue
27   should be "are we doing the right thing keeping that person alive?" or "are we doing
28   the right thing letting him die?"
29   In conclusion, I think the best thing to do is that each case should be reviewed
30   closely. If there's really no hope whatsoever of the patient recovering then it is more
31   merciful to let him die unless he expresses a desire to live; then his wishes should be
32   respected. Deciding whether a person should live or die is not easy—it is like taking
33   on the work of God.

Comments: Full, complete development of argument; can see both sides of the problem; gives plenty of supporting details. Organization and development are good: para. 1 restates both sides of the problem, without reusing the words of the prompt (assigned topic); para. 2 gives the circumstances under which one choice would be preferable, and the writer includes counter arguments (examples of arguments against the writer's opinion); para. 3 gives the circumstances under which a different choice would be preferable; para. 4 returns to a rephrasing of the opinions expressed in para. 2; and para. 5 summarizes the writer's position: to look at the specific circumstances of each situation before making a decision.

Fluent writing shows excellent range and control of grammar and vocabulary. Complex syntactic structures are used successfully: line 3, "on one hand" ties into line 5, "while on the other hand;" line 18 "in cases where" followed by line 19, "then it should be clear." Extensive embedding is used: line 5 "there are people who think"; line 25, "I can feel what it is like to be." Good use of hypotheticals ("if" clauses): lines 9, 15, 23, 30; and modals: lines 1 (should), 3 (must), 6 (should), 13 (might), etc. Vocabulary is broad and used appropriately: line 2, "controversial," "generated," line 3 "debate," line 9 "dignity," "recover," line 20 "expresses a desire," line 21 "wishes should be respected," line 22 "a very sorry thing," line 30 "recovering."

Essay 2

Score: 93. Full, clear development of theme. Fluent, complex, good vocabulary range. Should be as good as a native-speaker university student who does not have writing problems. Errors are few, sometimes native-type errors. Sometimes articles, or occasionally a preposition, that sound "foreign" but does not hinder reader's comprehension.

Topic: People who have been seriously injured, etc.

1   The basic issue involved here concerns human rights and more specifically, the right
2   to live. One has sole right to decide on his life, whether he wishes to live or to terminate
3   his 'miserable' life, provided he is considered normal enough i.e. he is not insane or
4   suffering from any disease which could obstruct human reasoning. In the movie "Whose
5   life is it anyway?", a paralysed man fought for his right to die but only after proven
6   perfectly capable of making a reasonable decisions as a human being. However, when
7   a victim is not consciously aware of himself or herself, then someone else must make
8   a decision. But who?
9   It all depends on whether the involved party has provided any instructions as to
10   what is to be done in case of such an emergency. Although this itself seemed highly
11   unlikely, it does seem sufficiently practical a solution to problems of similar nature!
12   Perhaps everyone should make it a rule to take such a precaution. Anyway the real
13   controversy is still unsolved yet.
14   Suppose a person is in an unconscious state of mind, maybe in a coma etc., and
15   incapable of decision-making while not 'saying' in advance in some selfpredetermined
16   manner his (or her) "final" wishes. Then it would be most appropriate to gather all
17   parties close to the victim (but only those who have a concrete idea of how the victim
18   would have decided, viz. spouse, parents and close friends) for a poll, a vote to make
19   the decision.
20   Otherwise let the jury decide it in court!

Comments: Good development of one side of the issue; might provide more general background in introduction. Good syntactic range: line 2 "whether he wishes to live or to terminate", lines 9–10, "depends on whether . . . as to what is to be done in case of"; line 15, "while not saying." Good control, only occasional errors which are not distracting: line 2 article deletion, "one has sole right," line 6 lack of agreement, "a reasonable decisions." Uses high level, sophisticated vocabulary: line 2, "terminate," line 5, "paralysed," line 11, "sufficiently," line 12, "precaution."

Essay 3

Score: 87. Full, clear development of theme. Meaning is clear, writing is fluent. Usually clearly organized; discourse-level and sentence-level syntax (grammatical structures) are good. Occasional article or preposition misuse or awkward phrase makes it obvious that the writer is a nonnative.

Topic: Discuss the advantages and disadvantages of having a part-time job instead of a full-time job.

1   For many people, holding a part-time job is terrible and unthinkable because they
2   think of its disadvantages only. To my mind, a part-time job offers disadvantages as
3   well as advantages.
4   The most valuable thing in life is time—it can not be bought. A part-time job allows
5   you much spare time for you to engage in other activities, important or unimportant
6   but necessary. If you are interested in writing, for example, you can write a lot during
7   your spare time, and one day in the future you may succeed. You can also study a
8   lot if you want; if you want to be a composer, you may have adequate time to make
9   music. Anyway, a part-time job will allow you some kind of concentration on doing
10   what you want to, while as a full-time job will keep you busy and tired—after you
11   come home after work, you are likely to have need of rest, then you can do little
12   during the very limited spare time. Again, because you work less hours for you part-
13   time job, you won't feel so tired and bored with your work. And you may have a
14   variety of activities in your life. However, a full-time job will keep you confined to
15   the workshop, if you're a worker, and you will become some sort of a machine yourself.
16   Men, after all, are not machines; they need something more besides making money
17   by working.
18   However, a part-time job doesn't make you earn much money which is needed for
19   daily necessities. Money sometimes allows you more freedom in your life. And, if you
20   have a family to support, it's inappropriate to have a part-time job only. You will feel
21   you're hard up for money, and that will perhaps affect your activities which might
22   lead to future success. Again, you don't have a job security if you have a part-time
23   job, and this may cause you worries. Anyway, for a person from a rich family, a part-
24   time job is excellent; for a poor person, it is not.

Comments: Well organized around a unifying principle (time is valuable, therefore a part-time job is good, because it allows you more time); includes another point of view in para. 3 (disadvantages of lack of money, job security).

Sometimes awkwardly expressed: in lines 2–3, the writer should put "advantages" before "disadvantages" to express his/her view to contrast with that of the "many people" who "think of disadvantages only" (lines 1–2); lines 12–13, "work...*for you* part-time job" could be corrected to "*at your* part-time job"; line 22 uses an unnecessary article, "*a* job security." Such errors of preposition choice and article use often appear at advanced proficiency levels. In general, though, the writing appears natural and fluent, and broad vocabulary is shown: line 8, "adequate," line 9, "concentration," line 19, "daily necessities."

Essay 4

Score: 83. Clear development of theme. Meaning is clear, writing is fluent. Variety of syntactic (sentence-level grammatical) structures used well, localized errors less numerous than at the 77 level. Transitions may not always be clearly indicated or smoothly achieved. Some, but not all of these characteristics may be present (i.e., errors take on an idiosyncratic character): vocabulary is basic, lacking specificity; there might be problems with prepositions, articles, some pronouns.

Topic: People who have been seriously injured, etc.

1   First of all, the point isn't the expense at all. We are lucky to live in a sociaty where
2   money can't be more important than keeping someone alive. However the matter is
3   much more difficult but in some other aspect. When someone is seriously injured and
4   then being kept alive by some machines, it's very important for me to know, whether
5   or not the patient is conscious. If he/she is conscious, according to my opinion, he/
6   she must be kept alive even by machines. As long you can still think, as long you can
7   still improve in your soul. You must be given the chance to live longer as long as it's
8   possible—I would like to emphasize once more than expenses may not count at all—
9   If you've became unconscious, and supposed you'll remain like that, the matter turns
10 to be much deeper, and much more difficult. According to the laws what all the doctors
11 have to follow they will keep you alive. The question overshows upon duty. The point
12 is whether or not they have the right for doing so or they don't. This has been discussed
13 for a long time and everybody has his individual opinion about it. I, personally was
14 working in several hospitals. I was a male nurse, an operating assistant, ambulance
15 attendant, I have been working with sick people for over four years. I've very much
16 experience, I was listening to diing people, I've heard lots of very interesting opinion
17 according to the matter, we are discussing now. And none of those opinions were the
18 same. The only resemblance was that you can choose from two answers "yes" or
19 "no". But the individual way on what these people tried to approach the question,
20 didn't even resemble one another. Once a man who was suffering with cancer and had
21 only a few days left told me that he wouldn't agree, supposed his condition would
22 turn even to worse, with keeping him alive by using any machines because he thinks
23 that he has the right—maybe the last one—to choose from suffering longer, or diing
24 in peace. I can't blame him. Once you get into a situation, and we all have to chance
25 to get there, what would you choose?
26   Well, this is one of the most difficult problem what many people were tring to

27 solve, but without result. This is a problem what can be solved only individually,
28 thereby everyone will come to his own conclusion. And, whatever that conclusion
29 would be, we all have to respect each an every answer, each and every solution.
30   The answers can depend on several factors. Eg. if the person is religious, he might
31 say . I, Although I suffer, I don't have to decide about my lif, what my God has given
32 to me"

Comment: The argument is developed fairly fully, and there is good use of detail (the writer draws from his experience in hospitals, lines 14–16, 20–24), but the organization isn't always clear, and the writer doesn't use enough paragraph markers. It could be improved by restating the problem at the beginning of the essay, rather than immediately starting with examples (lines 1, 3–5). There is good use of complex structures, though some errors occur at the local level. For example: lack of parallelism in sentence 3, lines 2–3; incorrect choice of relative pronoun in line 10, "what" for "that" or "which"; problems with word choice, line 11, "overshows," line 22, "turn" rather than "become"; lines 14–15, run-on sentence. Occasional spelling errors are not serious because they do not cause misunderstanding: line 1, "sociaty," line 31, "lif."

Essay 5

Another Example of an "83" Essay

Topic: Imagine you are in charge of establishing the first colony on the moon. What kind of people would you choose to take with you? What qualities and technical skills should they have?

1   If I were to in charge of establishing the first colony on the moon, I will not be too
2 picky about the characters of the people who I am going to take with me, but rather
3 I demand them to be enthusiastic about their lifes. Also, each of them should at least
4 have some skills in order to contribute in making a better land and society.
5   It is important for me to choose only those that are enthusiastic about their lifes
6 because I think these people will be willing to work hard and will set an aim to their
7 lifes. It is also because to establish a new colony requires hard working people. Those
8 who always like to eat and sleep just will not help.
9   Besides being enthusiastic, the people I will take with me must know some technical
10 skills. Doctors are the first on my list for I donot know conditions but there on the
11 moon, there may be diseases and my people may get affected. I will also bring with
12 me builders and architects to help to build houses, roads, hospitals etc. Professors and
13 school teachers will also be on my list for I will not want our next generation to be
14 illiterate. Also, I will bring some good cooks, and some dress-makers, in order to
15 allow my colony to be more modernized. Mechanics and technicians will also be on
16 my lists to help make light, electricity, etc.

Comment: Clearly addresses the topic (para. 1 states that the writer wants enthusiasm and technical skills rather than character, para. 2 discusses enthusiasm and para. 3 discusses technical skills), but lacks detail and full development. No summation is given at the end.

There is fairly good control of grammar and vocabulary (line 9, "Besides being enthusiastic"), with occasional minor errors (line 3, "lifes" [lives], line 4, "contribute *in* [towards] making," line 9, "*know* [have] technical skills").

Essay 6

Score: 77. The theme is clearly but not always fully developed. The writing is basically understandable and fluent. The writer knows and uses complex syntax (sentence-level grammar), but not without fairly frequent discrete morphological (localized) errors, *or* the writer may use only a limited syntactic range. There may be verb tense problems, confusion between use of active and passive voice. The vocabulary is usually appropriate, or a reasonable substitute for a more appropriate word, but may not always be highly specific. Often lacks discourse level connectors (such as "because," "since," "nevertheless," "moreover").

Topic: People who have been seriously injured, etc.

 1   Every human being has the right to live since they were to be born in this world.
 2   Nobody has the right to end their life just because they were coma, or could not be
 3   process anymore. In my opinion, I would say they should be kept alive, but also it
 4   depends on certain circumstances such as the most important thing is financial back-
 5   ground, also the age of the patient.
 6   Of course, a person who is going to spend most of his or her life on bed at the
 7   hospital and with a lots of help from doctor, nurses and also machine to keep him
 8   alive, it certainly need a large sum of money. If the victim came from a wealthy family
 9   and still young, his family should let him live because with all the efforts from doctors
 10   and medicine, probably after few months or few years later there is a changes for him
 11   to reborn again. If the victim is old, it is really a sad thing for him to suffer in the
 12   hospital. Death probably is the best way for him to go. However, if the victim came
 13   from a poor family background, his or her parents couldn't afford his hospital fees,
 14   mostly his has to end his life for the beneficial of his family.
 15   However, letting a person who is not really dead to die is a cruel thing to do. To
 16   certain people, they prefer to die rather than spending their whole life in the hospital
 17   and hoping for mysterious to come.

Comment: Good development of argument, tries to show several points of view. Good attempts at simple and complex syntax with subordination: lines 3–4, "I would say they should be . . . but also it depends on." However, there are frequent localized errors: line 3, "process"; line 6, "on bed"; line 7, "a lots of help"; line 8, "it certainly need"; line 10, "changes"; line 14, "beneficial." The overall syntax breaks down in para. 1, lines 3–5, and para. 2, lines 8–10. Sometimes the errors cause lack of clarity, and confusion in meaning: line 17, "hoping for mysterious to come."

Essay 7

Another "77" essay

Topic: People who have been seriously injured, etc.

1   The most horoble thing for someone would be to loose or injure a part from his or
2   her body. Such kind of people feel that the're missing something, there's something
3   wrong with them or they even go farther and think that they're worthless and useless.
4   If the most weight is on psychological problems then there ussualy can be found an
5   answer. Social workers, the family enviroment do their best.
6   The most difficult problems that we face are when a person has to stay all lifelong
7   becide or by the influence of some machine. What do we do? Let him live or help
8   him die? My personal opinion on this matter is let him live, No matter what it costs.
9   There is a life we're dealing with. That person has the right to live. But my question-
10 statement: Everything we think of people, is money? We should also keep them alive,
11 because there could be a chance that with the progress of Sciense, a cure may be
12 found for that certain disease.
13   Anyway we have an army of Scientists which are trying to find anything that can
14 be found; helpfull and destroyfull.
15   We have no right to allow someone to die unless he requests it. When the casualty
16 is consious and communicates and is able to understand and be understoud, and also
17 speak for himself then we should leave it up to him. He decides whether he wants to
18 live under those conditions, or he preffer diying than suffering and being a problem
19 to others.
20   Because we ussualy think and treat these people as a problem. The're not problems.
21 We could be in their case any time. Why are we called humans for? Letting our fellow
22 people to die because the cost or make our life a little uncomfortable?
23   The earn to live.

Comment: Fairly good command of structures, but breaks down in spots, and the meaning
is unclear, especially in the last two paragraphs. The writer tends to use simple syntactic
structures. The choice of transition or summary words (discourse markers) is not always
good: line 13, "Anyway." There are some problems with word choice: line 15, "casualty";
and word form: line 2, "the're"; line 14, "destroyfull." Spelling errors are frequent and
distracting but don't cause a breakdown in communication: line 1, "horoble," line 4,
"ussualy," line 5, "enviroment," line 11, "Sciense," line 16, "consious," line 18, "diying."

Essay 8

Score: 73. Theme not always fully developed, transitions might be incomplete or unclear.
Understandable without too much effort by the reader. Fluent in spots, but not necessarily
throughout. Simple sentence structures are successful, and attempts at complex structures
are made with some success. Many discrete (local) errors. Problems occur with pronouns,
relative clauses, sentence fragments, verbals. Basic vocabulary is usually adequate, but lacks
highly specific words.

Topic: Part-time instead of full-time job.

1   A part-time job has been getting popular recently. Not only the college students have
2   a part-time job, but also the housewives have a part-time job. Now, what are the
3   advantage and the disadvantage points about a part-time job?
4   First, I want to discuss about the advantage points. As for the college students, it
5   is good for them to get a part time job, because they get some money so that they
6   can enjoy their hobbies or save money. Furthermore, Having part-time-job is very
7   good experience for them, because they understand how difficult they get money by
8   themselves. As for the housewives, though they work in order to get better domestic
9   economic, that is also good for them to understand value of money.
10   Second, the disadvantage point of a part-time job; for example, the college students
11 who have their part-time job don't have time to study. That is the problem. And the
12 housewives who have their part-time job don't have time to take care of their children
13 and do their houseworks.
14   As a result, a part-time job is good for getting money, but affect on time.

Comment: This is well organized and clear, but shows limited development and language.
The organization is very clear: para. 1 states the popularity of part-time jobs for students
and housewives, then asks the rhetorical question about the advantages and disadvantages;
para. 2 describes some advantages for both students and housewives; para. 3 describes
some disadvantages, again for both students and housewives, and para. 4 is a one-sentence
summary. However, the theme is not fully developed, and the essay is very short. The writer
does not elaborate (explain in detail). While transition markers such as "First" (line 4)
and "Second" (line 10) are clear and help show organization, they are not as sophisticated
as other markers (such as "Initially," "Furthermore," "However, on the other hand") or
transition sentences would be. The syntax and vocabulary are also somewhat limited and
simple, though the meaning is clear.

Essay 9

Another "73" Essay.

Topic: People who have been seriously injured, etc.

1   Many things may happen to the people during their lives, and many injuries may come
2   to them. Also many children are born with many kindes of deseaces. Scientists are
3   studying whether to let these people to live as normal people or to getride of them
4   by sending them to death.
5   I think people who have been seriously injured and children who have been born with
6   serious gentic deseaces, must have the right to live there own lives, and there is no
7   choise for doctors or nay others people to end an injured men'slives. People should
8   be kept alive,even though it coast s agreat deal of maney. If doctors said the people
9   who injured allowed to die, he would interfer in the business of God. Because God
10 only can end Man's life.
11 The governments are sepending many to creat wars. Then after the wars end, there

12 must be many people who injoured during the war, therefore, governments oughts to
13 spend money for the victims of the wars. The governments must take care of those
14 injured people during the war.
15 And about children who were born with gentic deseaces the have the right to live and
16 no one can end their lives, because they were born in these condition for aporpos.
17 God wants to sea and examin the one who will be patient and strong facing the
18 problems. And God wants to reward these perons for his patience.
19 Finally the injured person also can't end his life for being injured because thise is the
20 life. One must face the problems and the meserable life very strongly and firmly. And
21 the govemments should spend alot of many to make those men feel better and live
22 abetter life—Because the govermments are fit first resporsible for there injury. The
23 Governmentscreat the proplems and the public afford the effects.

Comment: This is more fluent than the other "73" essay, and it uses more complex structures, but it has many more errors. The theme shows some development, and begins well by naming two types of ill people: those who have been injured and those who were born with diseases. The transitions and organization is not always clear, and lack of paragraph indentations makes it somewhat difficult to follow: para. 2 (lines 5–10) apparently concerns people with genetic diseases; then para. 3 (lines 11–14) at first appears unrelated, but eventually returns to injured people; and finally para. 4 (lines 15–18) unexpectedly returns to people with genetic diseases. The logic of para. 5 (lines 19–23) is not always clearly explained (why is the government responsible?). The writing is fairly fluent, and attempts complex syntax (lines 2–4, 5–7, 7–8), though there are run-on sentences and sentence fragments (lines 9–10, 15–16). Spelling and punctuation are poor, causing some confusion in meaning: line 3, "getride," line 16, "aporpos." Usually "73" essays will have better spelling and punctuation than this. Because of a combination of grammar, vocabulary, and spelling errors, some phrases are very difficult to understand: lines 19–20, "because thise is the life"; line 22, "the govermments are fit first resporsible"; line 23, "the public afford the effects."

Essay 10

Score: 67. Theme is not fully developed, transitions are incomplete or unclear. Understandable, but only with some effort by the reader; fluency is lacking. Most simple sentences are successful, but errors occur in attempts at complex structures. One particular syntactic (grammatical) structure may be used throughout. Many errors of all sorts.

Topic: Moon colony.

1 If I were in charge of establishing the first colony on the moon, I would take my
2 husband, a doctor, a nurse and a artchiteture.
3 If I wanted to create a new world, I should create humans If I did not bring my
4 husband with. How could I create humans? There was no people on the moon for
5 even.
6 If the humans were create on the moon, it was improtant for them to have a medicine
7 care. Everyone would be sick at any time. When they are sick, they have to consult

a doctor. It was improtant for me to bring a doctor and a nurse. It was because I
9   wanted to create the human. If I gave birth, no people knew how to take care of me.
10   If I died, who would create the human on the moon?

11   I lived on the moon. There is a lot of space. I could built a big house. Thus, I
12   could live comfortably. Hence, I needed to bring a artchiteture. The artchiteture would
13   design a suitable house for me.

14   When I were in change of world, I would need electronic skill. Even on the moon,
15   It has a day and night. During a night time, it is very dark. I could not do anything.
16   I needed a light. If I did not have electronic skill, I would not have a light for even.
17   All the thing I could is sleep during the night.

18   Also, I could bring a plane Although I created the human on the moon, I had to
19   go back to the earth to visit my family. It was convinence for me to visit them if I
20   had plane. I could go back every time I liked.

21   I had to bring the cooking skills. Although I lived in the moon. It didn't means I
22   did not need to eat anything I ate food in order to have energy. If I did not know
23   how to cook, I just would drink some water and eat the raw food for even. Hence,
24   I would died very soon. Therefore, cooking skills were improtant for me.

Comment: Basically, limited with many errors. This is a rather low 67, because the structures
used are so basic and limited. No overall organizing principle is given. The organization
begins adequately, but then breaks down. There are no transitions between paragraphs,
and no hierarchy (ordering from most important to least important) of ideas is present.
Para. 1 begins with people to bring to the colony, and lists husband, doctor, nurse, and
"artchiteture" (architect). Then para. 2 briefly explains the necessity of the husband, para.
3, that of the doctor and nurse, and para. 4, that of the architect. After this, the organization
becomes unclear, and seems to be only a list of ideas. Structurally, there are many simple
sentences (lines 11, 15, 16, 21). The writer lacks control of complex structures, and there
are many verb tense problems, especially with hypotheticals ("if" clauses) and modals.
Lines 1–2 show successful use of the hypothetical, but in line 6 the wrong verb is used
("*was* important" rather than "would be"), in line 3 the wrong modal is used ("should"
rather than "would" or "would have to"), and in line 9 the wrong verb is used again ("if
I gave birth, no people *knew,*" rather than "would know.") Spelling errors are distracting,
and sometimes slow the reader (lines 16 and 23, "even" instead of "ever").

Essay 11

Another "67" Essay

Topic: People who have been seriously injured, etc.

1   The medicine in the world is preceeding quickly and the purpose of that is only to
2   protect the human-being, and in the same time we cann't evaluate the human being
3   by money, and I know that the machines designed for keeping the people who injured
4   or any thing else alive. In my opinion if I have to choose between paying a lot of
5   money to save a person or leave him die I,ll choose the first one, just for one reasen
6   because if the person works he can get money but its imposible to create a person by

7   the machines.
8   In the other way if the person who injured cann't pay to save himself The goverment
9   of his country has to take care of these problems because in any way The hospitals
10   who take care of these persons has a lot of expenses for that htis problem has to be
11   solved already by high responsibles or governors, because the human being has to stay
12   the most important thing in this life.
13   There is another thing the people can do it to establish or to create a big associations
14   to take care of the poor people and to handle them with a kid gloves because all times
15   they need helping and surrerring from the high class of people.

Comment: This writer tries more complex language, but the writing is error-ridden. The
argument is not always clear, especially in para. 2, lines 8–12, regarding the explanation
of why the government should pay. There are some problems with logic, as in lines 6 and
7, where the connection between machines and money is not clear. There are problems with
sentence structure: run-on sentences appear in lines 4–7, and para. 2, lines 8–12. A sentence
fragment appears in line 4. Subordination is not always successful or is not used where it
should be (lines 10–11). There are some inappropriate lexical (word choice) problems: line
8, "In the other way," rather than "on the other hand"; and line 11 "responsibles," for
"authorities"; one lexical item is incomprehensible: line 15, "surrerring." Nonetheless, some
use of high level vocabulary is shown: line 1, "preceeding," line 2, "evaluate."

Essay 12

Another "67" Essay

Topic: Moon colony.

1   The kind of peiple to be choosen would be, the ones that in one way or another hard
2   show How weel, and Responsably they are. go to the moon is a factor of behaverr
3   and the people that is going to enjoy that colony have to have not just good actituds
4   but also education and be able get command.
5   They wiil be able to remaind calm by the time it may would be reguaire they will
6   need to have a high level in any kind of technical skills and those may be, computer,
7   food, ecology etc. this people will be the ones to live in there, will be no Rivers, walks
8   in the park or anything like that, so they would need to be prepare mentally and
9   fisically to this new experience. No body is going to help them, becouse they would
10   be far away from they original planet, also they will need to live as one becouse
11   lonliness may be a factor.
12   Establishing a new colony in the moom maigh take a cople years but by the time
13   it come we will be rady becouse since now, education is been giving, and young people
14   are the gnes in the way of learning. The future is greate and so is the aportuinity, our
15   future knites of the mood will be the first step forward to gain the space, and travel
16   arround the hold universe will be like go for a Ride in one sundy morning.
17   The futur aritauts of the moon will be the ones to get the will of the human Race,
18   and theryore they are goinng to be blacks, chineses, Spanish etc people for all arraind
19   the world, will enjoy this cruse, with the jope of create love, respect, and confidence

20   in every one of them, ones againg, they wil need to work as a group in order to

21   survive, and put all their technical skills together in order to make so anelate gold.

Comment: The writer attempts complex structures and phrases but with many errors: lines 12–14 show good overall structure but have frequent localized errors. Some inappropriate word choice is shown: line 1, "hard," line 2, "factor," line 13, "giving." Some incorrect word forms are used: line 2, "Responsably." The frequent spelling errors are distracting, and tend to impede comprehension because of their frequency and severity: line 2, "weel," line 3, "actituds," line 5, "reguaire," line 12, "maigh," line 17, "aritauts," line 18, "arraind."

Essay 13

Score: 63. Theme undeveloped, unclear. Sometimes short. May be difficult to understand. Has control over some simple sentences and limited vocabulary.

Topic: Moon colony.

1   First that all, I need The perfect conditions for your lives. This conditions are for

2   example: houses, stores, medical center and other places, but for this places is nec-

3   cessary their construction. I need people with this technical, equipment and people

4   ables in enroller this group, this people are youngers and with a good capacity for to

5   do your work.

6   In other words, I need people with experience in give and reciber orders.

7   When the construction is finished with the places readys I need people of each profession

8   of both sexs for your completion and necesary.

9   All the places will have a good conditions for comfort the each person and all people

10   will have theirselves satisfaction. In this colony will have a lot communications, because

11   whole people will be friendly, and generous.

12   This communications are for example: radio, TV, telephone, and a lot roads.

13   In the comfort, they will have restaurant,. place for enjoy, for example parks, disck

14   and other places.

15   The economic in my colony is very cheap, because the foot was around of the

16   agriculture.

17   The people will use the sun for the electricity and the water for evaporation of lage

18   and then a recicle.

19   All of the waste willbe procces and recicle.

20   All them leaving in peace.

Comment: Lacks an overall organizing principle; mostly lists with no dominant theme. Frequently confusing to the reader. Communication would have been improved if the writer had indented paragraphs, thus helping signal transitions to the reader. Some conditions of living on the moon are given: para. 3, houses and comfort, para. 5, communications, para. 6, restaurant, para. 7, economy (not explained), and para. 8, power source. However, none are tied together under any organizing idea or theme. Short sentence structures are fairly successful, but many words are out of order (e.g., lines 9–10). Frequently the wrong word form is used: line 13, "enjoy," line 15, "economic." Word choices are not used well: line

1, "that," line 11, "whole people." Pronouns are used incorrectly in a way that confuses the reader: "your" in lines 1, 5, and 8.

Essay 14

Another "63" Essay

Topic: People who have been seriously injured, etc.

1 Poeple come to leaf to live, for this reason we should try as hard as possible to keep
2 them alive. If we sign dwon to allowed them to die, this mistake we will never forget.
3 In my opoin, to take part in dision of allowing someone to death, even if her or she
4 seriously injured, is the same as to kill someone in a good health. These machines
5 which the human event it should take part in saving the other leafs.
6 We might be mean for a person or other, but being mean in saving someone leaf is
7 a crime. Why we have to store our money in banks although we all know that the
8 money come and go and no one can be sure that his money will remain with him
9 until he die.
10 In case I do not have any money,and in the same time my borther or sister or any
11 one of my relative is suffering from his serious enjured do I have to watch or allowed
12 him to die? even though I have a good reeson to allowed him to die I won't do it. I
13 might work in another jobe beside mine, ask friends for help ask any bank or organ-
14 ization for lending me the money I need.
15 I have to do my duty in the best way I can.Human leaf is not an easy thing to be
16 send to death.Every one in the world should do his best to save someone from death.

The argument is not clear, and transitions are poor. There are serious syntactic errors (lines 4–5, 6–7) and spelling errors (line 2, "dwon," line 3, "opoin," "dision") which impede communication (make it difficult to understand). Language problems cause confusion in spots (sentences in lines 4–5, and lines 6–7), so that the meaning is unclear.

Essay 15

Score: 57. Theme is undeveloped and unclear. Short, fairly incomprehensible, some recognizable phrases. General meaning can be gotten with rereading.

Topic: A good friend of yours asks for advice about whether to go to work and make money or whether to continue school. What advice would you give him/her?

I'm glad to write you. I've knew that you are going to U.S. to continue your education. But I don't know what you are ready for it. If fact I know, you have good conditions for our study. Because that you have good basic in English Language and you study very hard I know. Howeaver, you have to take a Michigan Test or TOEFL TEST, then you can find a College or University which you interest in. you must hand in your application form and good scores of Michigan Test or TOEFL. Besides, you have to through much red type in other way.

Comment: Very short and undeveloped. Limited syntax and vocabulary. Some basic information conveyed. Fairly good accuracy for a "57" level essay.

Essay 16

Score: 53. Short and incomprehensible; single words may be recognizable.

Topic: Discuss the advantages and disadvantages of having a part-time job instead of a full-time job.

> If I gose to U.S.A. I'll like to having a part-time job. becuose I sbjact will sdudy to play piano with go to U.S.A. I'll to sdudy it for need morn time. but not a job. my life could have defficalty.

Comment: Extremely short and undeveloped. The topic is never really addressed. The meaning is nearly incomprehensible, and idea(s) are unclear. General syntax, grammar, and vocabulary limitations and errors make it difficult to understand.

Part 2: Listening

Introduction

The listening test is designed to show how well you understand spoken English, as used by native speakers of English. The test itself is played on an audio tape recording. You will be given a test booklet and separate answer sheet. The test booklet contains printed instructions and answer choices for the listening test. You should mark all your answers on the separate answer sheet. You will hear the instructions on the tape recording as you read them in the test booklet. You will also hear several examples. The examiner will pause the recording after the instructions and examples have been played to see if you have any questions about how to do the test and to see if sound adjustments need to be made. Once the test begins, however, none of the actual test problems will be repeated. The entire test will contain about 50 problems and will take about 25 minutes.

If you have a hearing problem, you should tell the examiner *before* the date of the test, so that special seating arrangements or a special administration can be arranged. You should be prepared to bring to the test a written document from a medical doctor confirming your hearing problem.

With beginning level students, English as a Second Language (ESL) teachers modify (change) their speech in class. They often speak more slowly and enunciate (pronounce) more carefully in class than they do when they are talking to other native speakers of English. If you have never heard native speakers of English talking to each other, this test may surprise you. It seems to nonnative speakers of any language that the native speakers speak very quickly. It may also seem that words "run together," that is, they are spoken in phrases rather than a single word at a time, with deliberate pauses between words. For example, in conversational English, many contractions occur. A short question like "How would you like to go for a walk?" may sound like "How'dja liketa gofra walk?"

Two good ways to become accustomed to native English speakers is to speak with them, if possible, and to listen to radio and television broadcasts. Several publishing companies in the United States sell teaching materials that include audio tapes for listening comprehension practice. Appendix D lists study materials for listening practice.

The listening test section of the MELAB is entirely multiple choice. It contains:

1. Short questions. You should choose the appropriate response (a reasonable answer to the question).
2. Short statements or dialogues. You should choose the appropriate paraphrase or summary. This is a statement that means about the same thing as what the speaker(s) said.

3. Short statements in which certain words are emphasized. You should choose an appropriate continuation of the statement.
4. A longer monologue (one person giving a short lecture) and a dialogue (a conversation between two people). During the lecture and dialogue, you may take notes on your answer sheet. Following the lecture and dialogue, you will be asked content questions about them, and you may refer to your notes to answer the questions.

After each problem or question in the test, you will be allowed 12–15 seconds to read the answer choices and choose your answer. More time will be allowed for problems with longer written answers cr for problems that require you to refer to your notes.

During this test, it is important to concentrate and listen carefully to what you hear. During the short question and statement parts, look at the answer choices as you listen to the question or statement. Then quickly choose an answer and mark it on your answer sheet. If you miss a question or don't understand it, quickly guess at the answer and mark your choice. Then you will be ready for the next question. During the lecture and conversation, do not look at the answer choices, but listen carefully and write important points or details on the space provided on the answer sheet. After the lecture or conversation, you will hear questions. Choose the best answer from the choices printed in the test booklet. You may refer to your notes if necessary. Mark your answer choices on the separate answer sheet. Remember, none of the problems in the test will be repeated.

Examples of Listening Test Problems

Here is an example of the short question type of problem.
    You will hear:

"Example I: When's she going on vacation?"

You will read in your test booklet:

Ex. I a. Last week.
        b. To England.
        c. Tomorrow.

The correct answer is *c, tomorrow,* because that is the best response to the question. The speaker asked *when,* so a time expression is needed in the answer. Also, the present continuous tense (as "she is going") is often used to express future tense, so you know she has not gone on her vacation yet.
    Here is an example of the short statement type of problem. You should choose the statement that means about the same thing as what you hear.
    You will hear:

(Male voice): "Example II: That movie was pretty bad."
(Female voice): "It sure was!"

You will read in your test booklet:

Ex. II   a. She disagrees that it was good.
         b. She agrees that it wasn't good.
         c. She agrees that it was beautiful.

The correct answer is *b, She agrees that it wasn't good.* His statement means the movie was bad, not good. Here "bad" is modified by "pretty." "Pretty" is used for emphasis, like "very," here, "pretty" doesn't mean nice looking.

Here is an example of the emphasis type of problem. You will hear a statement that is spoken in a certain way, with special emphasis. The word may be emphasized by being spoken louder, or with a pause before or after it. You should listen for the emphasis and interpret it. Choose the answer that tells what the speaker would probably say next:
You will hear:

"Example III: I needed the *small* red cup."

You will read in your test booklet:

Ex. III   The speaker would continue...
          a. not the big one.
          b. not the green one.
          c. not the plate.

The correct answer is *a, not the big one,* because the speaker emphasized the word *small.* The speaker was emphasizing the size of the cup, contrasting the small with the large one. If the speaker had wanted to emphasize the color of the cup, the word *red* would have been emphasized, and choice *b, not the green one* would have been correct.

When you hear the emphasis problems, listen for the word that is emphasized. Then classify it as a noun, adjective, verb, etc. Then, choose the answer in the same class. Here, an adjective (small) describing size is emphasized. "Big" in answer choice *a* is also an adjective describing the size of an object. Big contrasts with small. In choice *b,* green is also an adjective, but it describes color, not size. In choice *c,* plate is a noun.

In the actual test, you will not be given an example of the lecture or dialogue problems. Here are some suggestions for what to listen for:

As you listen to the lecture, try to decide the main idea. This will usually be emphasized by repetition. The lecturer might say, "This is a key issue," or, "This is an important point." Next, decide what the lecturer's supporting arguments are. These might be examples used to illustrate the main idea. The lecturer might say, "for instance," or "for example," or, "to illustrate this point." The lecturer may have an opinion that he or she contrasts with someone else's opinion. Listen for transition words and phrases, such as "first," "next," "let's turn to," "let's move on to," "to summarize," "finally." "But" is often used to signal the transition from one idea to another. These are organization markers.

As you listen to the dialogue, ask yourself what the relationship of the two speakers is. This might not give you any direct answers to the questions that follow, but it may help you to understand the conversation and the setting. Do the speakers know each other?

Are they old friends? Are they strangers to each other? Where do you think they are talking: on the street? on a telephone? in an office or store? What information do they give each other? Do they give directions to locate something? instructions on how to do something? Often, after someone gives instructions or directions, the other person will repeat them to confirm that he or she understands them. Do they express opinions about other people or circumstances? Do they agree or disagree? Do they sometimes misunderstand each other? As a listener, you understand better if you have a good idea of what you *expect* to hear. If you understand the theme or main idea of the conversation and what the relationship of the speakers is, you will understand the whole conversation better. The dialogue will not be as well organized as the lecture, and there probably won't be any transition or organization markers. Sometimes the speakers may digress (go away) from the main subject.

Practice Listening Tests

Here are two practice tests. Before you begin the practice tests, review the examples just given. An answer key and a script for the practice tests are on pp. 75–99, but do not look at them yet.

First, take the practice test. Answer sheets for the two listening tests are in appendix E in the back of this book. Play the tape recording straight through, without stopping or repeating any of the questions. Then score your test using the key. You may take the test in this way several times, if you wish, but be sure you use a new answer sheet each time.

Next, you should score your test using the key. Finally, review the practice test by playing the tape recording as you read the script. Compare your answers with those in the key. At this time, you may stop the recording and repeat questions if you wish.

Do *not* look at the key or script until you have taken the entire test at least once and have marked your answers on the answer sheet. If you look at the key or script too soon, you cannot make an accurate assessment of your listening ability, and your score will not be correct or interpretable.

Part 2, Practice Test 1

Before you begin this practice test, review the examples. Do *not* look at the key or script until you have finished the entire test.

This test contains several kinds of problems. There are short questions, for which you should choose the appropriate answer or reply. There are short statements and dialogues, for which you should choose the appropriate paraphrase or summary. There are short statements, in which certain words are emphasized. For these you should choose an appropriate continuation of the statement, that is, what the speaker would probably say next. Finally, there will be a lecture and longer conversation. During the lecture and conversation, you may take notes on your answer sheet. After the lecture and conversation, you will be asked questions about them.

Here is an example of the short question type of problem.

    Ex. I   a. Last week.
            b. To England.
            c. Tomorrow.

The correct answer is *c, Tomorrow,* because that is the best response to the question. Choice *c* has been marked on your answer sheet to show that it is the correct answer.

   Here is an example of the short statement type of problem. You should choose the statement that means about the same thing as what you heard.

    Ex. II   a. She disagrees that it was good.
             b. She agrees that it wasn't good.
             c. She agrees that it was beautiful.

The correct answer is *b, She agrees that it wasn't good,* because that means about the same thing as the statements. Choice *b* has been marked on your answer sheet for example II.

Here is an example of the emphasis type of problem. You will hear a statement that is spoken in a certain way, with special emphasis. You should listen for the emphasis and interpret it. Choose the answer that tells what the speaker would probably say next.

    Ex. III   a. not the big one.
              b. not the green one.
              c. not the plate.

The correct answer is *a, not the big one,* because the speaker emphasized the word *small.* Choice *a* has been marked on your answer sheet for example III. Now we will begin Practice Test 1. Turn the page to problem 1.
For problems 1–12, choose the appropriate response to the question.

1. a. In Sue's car.
   b. Sue's parents are.
   c. Before noon.

2. a. See a movie.
   b. I'd like to.
   c. Steak and potatoes.

3. a. Yes, I've been there twice.
   b. No, it's about twice as expensive.
   c. No, it takes twice as long.

4. a. Not in the office.
   b. At 2 o'clock.
   c. My last test.

5. a. Yes, I do.
   b. No, she doesn't.
   c. Yes, she will.

6. a. Yes, you can use them.
   b. No, you don't.
   c. Because yours aren't any better.

7. a. Make a special appointment with me.
   b. My office is in room 203.
   c. My office hours are from 9 to 11.

8. a. If you want to.
   b. No, I'm not.
   c. Yes, I'm finished.

9. a. Late last night.
   b. Sounds like fun.
   c. They'll go with you.

10. a. The river flooded.
    b. When it rained last night.
    c. It might have.

11. a. Near Central Park.
    b. The subway.
    c. Straight down 5th Avenue.

12. a. He wasn't here.
    b. In order to get them.
    c. For the secretary.

For problems 13–28, choose the answer that means about the same thing as the statement or short dialogue you hear.

13. a. Mary did the work.
    b. Mary needs help.
    c. Mary left on time.

14. a. He arrived after it started.
    b. He arrived before it started.
    c. He arrived after it ended.

15. a. Jane didn't go to London.
    b. Jane will go to London.
    c. Jane likes big cities.

16. a. We don't get anything done.
    b. We need more work to do.
    c. We get some things done.

17. a. He buys her groceries.
    b. She buys him groceries.
    c. She buys her own groceries.

18. a. She's here now.
    b. She's coming soon.
    c. She comes often.

19. a. His brothers finished it.
    b. Tom finished it.
    c. They all finished it.

20. a. John should add them first.
    b. John should check them first.
    c. John should make a record first.

21. a. He won't sell it.
    b. He will sell it.
    c. He'll think about it.

22. a. He had forgotten it.
    b. He left it at work.
    c. He'll get there soon.

23. a. He got the money.
    b. He was released from prison.
    c. He's no longer in prison.

24. a. He doesn't look so old.
    b. He is always overlooked.
    c. The man read the books.

25. a. Smith's students are quiet.
    b. Smith doesn't have many students.
    c. Smith has many students.

26. a. He can fix the broken equipment.
    b. He'll replace her for a while.
    c. He'll take it there for her.

27. a. He doesn't need to take anything.
    b. She can register him now.
    c. He should take some identification.

28. a. They think the discussion was useful.
    b. They're having an argument.
    c. They'll leave together.

The next problems are of the emphasis type. For problems 29–36, choose the answer that is what the speaker would probably say next.

29. The speaker would continue...
    a. not Dad.
    b. not for lunch.
    c. not beef.

30. The speaker would continue...
    a. not her camping trip.
    b. not the last two.
    c. not Elizabeth.

31. The speaker would continue...
    a. not tomorrow.
    b. not at work.
    c. not your father.

32. The speaker would continue...
    a. not the green ones.
    b. not the placemats.
    c. not put away.

33. The speaker would continue...
    a. not moved there.
    b. not all summer.
    c. not Rome.

34. The speaker would continue...
    a. not painted.
    b. not doors.
    c. not requiring it.

35. The speaker would continue...
    a. but not to do his work.
    b. but Joe doesn't have time.
    c. but not enough money.

36. The speaker would continue...
    a. not go there.
    b. not the head manager.
    c. It's Tom's job.

Now you will hear a lecture. As you listen, you may take notes about the lecture. Write the notes on your answer sheet. After the lecture is finished, you will be asked some questions about it.

37. a. polluted water
    b. fewer shellfish
    c. traffic jams, more houses and boats

38. a. traffic jams, more houses and boats
    b. changes in marine fauna
    c. closed beaches

39. a. Water becomes polluted.
    b. Clams become polluted and can't be eaten.
    c. The number of marine fauna species is reduced.

40. a. land development
    b. high bacteria counts
    c. a stressed environment

41. a. It has died off.
    b. It is so polluted it can't be eaten.
    c. It can't be used as a seed clam.

42. a. Beaches are closed to swimmers.
    b. Clams and fish have died off.
    c. The beachfront is crowded with houses and boats.

43. a. 75 percent will live within fifty miles of an ocean or the Great Lakes.
    b. 50 percent will live within seventy-five miles of an ocean or the Great Lakes.
    c. Those living in the Northeast will have the greatest problems.

Now you will hear a conversation between two people. As you listen, you may take notes on your answer sheet. After the conversation, you will be asked some questions about it.

44. a. They weren't familiar with the area.
    b. To be sure of a place to stay at night.
    c. They wanted to save money.

45. a. postcards
    b. spoons
    c. a teacup

46. a. #7
    b. #9
    c. #12

47. a. the gardens
    b. the museum
    c. the Cheese Board

48. a. All their activities would be planned for them.
    b. They might not find a place to stay at night.
    c. They might not have money for dinner.

49. a. Mercer's Antiques
    b. the Cheese Board
    c. the farm museum

50. a. They have a larger selection.
    b. They're convenient and cheaper.
    c. They're more crowded and expensive.

End Practice Test 1.

Part 2, Practice Test 2

Before you begin this practice test, review the examples. Do *not* look at the key or script until you have finished the entire test.

This test contains several kinds of problems. There are short questions, for which you should choose the appropriate answer or reply. There are short statements and dialogues, for which you should choose the appropriate paraphrase or summary. There are short statements, in which certain words are emphasized. For these you should choose an appropriate continuation of the statement, that is, what the speaker would probably say next. Finally, there will be a lecture and longer conversation. During the lecture and conversation, you may take notes on your answer sheet. After the lecture and conversation, you will be asked questions about them.

Here is an example of the short question type of problem.

> Ex. I   a. Last week.
>   b. To England.
>   c. Tomorrow.

The correct answer is *c, Tomorrow,* because that is the best response to the question. Choice *c* has been marked on your answer sheet to show that it is the correct answer.

Here is an example of the short statement type of problem. You should choose the statement that means about the same thing as what you heard.

> Ex. II   a. She disagrees that it was good.
>   b. She agrees that it wasn't good.
>   c. She agrees that it was beautiful.

The correct answer is *b, She agrees that it wasn't good,* because that means about the same thing as the statements. Choice *b* has been marked on your answer sheet for example II.

Here is an example of the emphasis type of problem. You will hear a statement that is spoken in a certain way, with special emphasis. You should listen for the emphasis and interpret it. Choose the answer that tells what the speaker would probably say next.

> Ex. III   a. not the big one.
>   b. not the green one.
>   c. not the plate.

The correct answer is *a, not the big one,* because the speaker emphasized the word *small.* Choice *a* has been marked on your answer sheet for example III. Now we will begin Practice Test 2. Turn the page to problem 1.

For problems 1–10, choose the appropriate response to the question.

1. a. No, I don't think you can.
   b. If you want to.
   c. At the end of the hall.

2. a. Maybe he came to the party.
   b. If he's not busy.
   c. Yes, he gave them to me.

3. a. Sure, I'll do it.
   b. After I go to the cleaners.
   c. On my way home.

4. a. It's hard to say.
   b. Yes, she can improve it.
   c. No, I can't prove it.

5. a. I take the bus.
   b. My brother told me how.
   c. I enjoy it.

6. a. Sorry, I'm not going to class.
   b. Sorry, I don't mind.
   c. Yes, please give it to her.

7. a. Yes, Mary has.
   b. No, I can't.
   c. Yes, it was late.

8. a. Sure, no problem.
   b. At my office.
   c. On Friday.

9. a. It's quite important.
   b. 50 words per minute.
   c. Open it quickly.

10. a. Do the writing first.
    b. Both of them will.
    c. OK, I'll go there first.

For problems 11–28, choose the answer that means about the same thing as the statement or short dialogue you hear.

11. a. They went home at 6 o'clock.
    b. They practiced more than 6 hours.
    c. They are still practicing.

12. a. He liked the party.
    b. He doesn't like parties.
    c. He didn't go to the party.

13. a. My news pleased them.
    b. My news surprised them.
    c. Their news bothered me.

14. a. It's better if they wait.
    b. They should go soon.
    c. They were 5 minutes late.

15. a. He didn't go to the Capitol Building.
    b. He visited the Capitol Building.
    c. He didn't visit Washington.

16. a. We like living there.
    b. We used to live there.
    c. It was like home to us.

17. a. He didn't wear one.
    b. He did wear one.
    c. He will wear one.

18. a. I want to stay at your house.
    b. I want you to keep my car.
    c. I went away on vacation.

19. a. I liked the way he looked.
    b. I didn't like the way he looked.
    c. I didn't like the way he acted.

20. a. He should do it.
    b. He needs it.
    c. He probably did it.

21. a. John is working outside.
    b. John likes his job.
    c. John exercises at work.

22. a. A raise was given.
    b. A raise will probably be given.
    c. Large profits aren't expected.

23. a. We wrote a letter.
    b. She did it alone.
    c. She was helped.

24. a. He solved it.
    b. He finished it.
    c. He explained it.

25. a. Betty is gone.
    b. Betty is afraid to leave.
    c. Betty is going to leave.

26. a. He's moving now.
    b. He'll help for an hour.
    c. He can't help her now.

27. a. They got incorrect information.
    b. They don't know when Richards will arrive.
    c. They know Richards' arrival time.

28. a. He can't do it in a week.
    b. He did it a week ago.
    c. He'll probably need a week.

The next problems are of the emphasis type. For problems 29–37, choose the answer that tells what the speaker would probably say next.

29. The speaker would continue...
    a. not flying.
    b. not Chicago.
    c. not today.

30. The speaker would continue...
    a. not two.
    b. not a small one.
    c. not vanilla.

31. The speaker would continue...
    a. not their writing skills.
    b. not the teachers.
    c. not the university.

32. The speaker would continue...
    a. not the radio.
    b. not just repair it.
    c. not you.

33. The speaker would continue...
    a. not too large.
    b. not for Robert.
    c. not the sweater.

34. The speaker would continue...
    a. not sometimes.
    b. not Harry's.
    c. not my bicycle.

35. The speaker would continue...
    a. Ellen wrote him.
    b. Ellen told Martha.
    c. Martha told him.

36. The speaker would continue...
    a. not to ride.
    b. not the zoo.
    c. not around it.

37. The speaker would continue...
    a. not the letter.
    b. not demanded.
    c. not write it.

Now you will hear a lecture. As you listen, you may take notes about the lecture. Write the notes on your answer sheet. After the lecture is finished, you will be asked some questions about it.

38. a. a bunch of daffodils
    b. radiographs of flowers
    c. a visit to a five and dime store

39. a. black and white photography
    b. a purely dental technique
    c. X-ray photography

40. a. They are recorded on X-ray film.
    b. They are in black and white.
    c. They reflect light onto radiographs.

41. a. yield black and white images
    b. record reflected transmitted light
    c. penetrate X-rays

42. a. X-rays penetrate the subject
    b. X-rays reflect transmitted light
    c. X-rays don't require light

43. a. They reflect light.
    b. They are black and white.
    c. They are transparent.

Now you will hear a telephone conversation. As you listen, you may take notes on your answer sheet. After the conversation, you will be asked some questions about it.

44. a. No limit, but they must be returned in six weeks.
    b. No limit, but they must be returned in two weeks.
    c. Six books every two weeks.

45. a. Saturday mornings
    b. Friday evenings
    c. weekday afternoons

46. a. East Fork
    b. Miller Road
    c. Ballou Road

47. a. Saturday mornings
    b. Friday mornings
    c. weekday afternoons

48. a. A notice is mailed to parents.
    b. They're posted in the IGA food market.
    c. They're advertised in the *Town Crier.*

49. a. go straight
    b. go north
    c. go east

50. a. a blinking light
    b. the food market
    c. the library

End Practice Test 2.

Part 3: Grammar, Cloze, Vocabulary, Reading

This part of the MELAB battery has four different kinds of problems: grammar, cloze reading, vocabulary, and reading comprehension. If you take a 100-item test, the time limit is 75 minutes (1 hour and 15 minutes); if the test is longer, e.g., 130 or 144 items, the time limit will be extended accordingly. When you take this part of the test, it is important to answer the problems as quickly as you can. Do not spend a great deal of time on individual grammar or vocabulary problems; remember that the reading will take longer because you must read a paragraph in addition to answering questions about it. Look for the right answer, or one that seems correct, rather than looking at all the answers and trying to eliminate the wrong ones. Often, two answers will seem correct while the other two are clearly wrong. Choose the most likely, and lightly circle the item number on your answer sheet (if you have a machine-scannable answer sheet, you should not do this, or you should go back and erase all such marks). If you have time at the end of the test, you can go back and spend more time on the problems you were unsure of. If you do not know the answer, guess. You are not penalized for guessing: your final score is based on the total number of correct answers.

For the grammar problems, you should review word order in statements, questions and embedded phrases, noun compounds, prepositions, connectors, adverbs and adjectives, verb tenses, subject-verb agreement, use of active and passive voice, modals, infinitives, and gerunds. Though the grammar problems are in a conversational format, they include some formal as well as informal usage. About half the grammar problems will concern verbs.

Here is an example of a grammar problem. You should choose the word or phrase that correctly completes the conversation.

"How did you know that Helen was here?"
"She _____ by some of her friends."
   a. seen
   b. is seeing
   c. has seen
   d. was seen

The correct answer is *d, was seen*. This is the passive past tense form of the verb "to see." Passive voice must be used because the friends are the ones who saw Helen, who is the subject of the sentence, and past tense should be used because the action (Helen was seen) took place in the past.

In the cloze reading section, you will read a paragraph from which 20 words have been deleted (taken out). You should choose, from the choices given, the one word that fits each blank both in grammar and in meaning. Skim quickly through the cloze passage to get the main idea before you try to select the correct words for the blanks. As you skim the cloze passage, think of what word form fits each blank (noun, adjective, verb, connector, etc.), and think of a meaning that might fit before you look at the answer choices. Be sure to read the entire sentence that the missing word appears in; an incorrect choice may seem to fit in a phrase, but will not fit in the context of the whole sentence. You might get some clues to a missing word in the sentence that comes before or after it. The missing word will usually not be a difficult or unusual word; if it is unusual, you can probably guess it from the context of the cloze passage.

Here is an example of a short cloze passage.

In years to come, zoos will not only be places where animals are exhibited to the public, but repositories where rare species can be saved from extinction __(1)__ captive breeding. The most powerful force __(2)__ the future of many animals—and of zoos—is the decline of the wild. __(3)__ even zoo directors would argue that __(4)__ are better places for animals than the fields and forests of their native __(5)__ , yet zoos may be the last chance for some creatures that would otherwise pass quietly into oblivion.

1. a. through   c. from
   b. of   d. damage
2. a. bringing   c. to
   b. that   d. influencing
3. a. But   c. Not
   b. So   d. Then
4. a. where   c. even
   b. zoos   d. wilds
5. a. lands   c. residence
   b. life   d. field

The correct answers are: 1*a*, 2*d*, 3*c*, 4*b*, 5*a*. For 1, a preposition that means "by means of" is needed as a sentence-level connector. For 2, a verb that means "affecting" is needed. For 3, you need to read ahead in the sentence to understand that zoo officials do *not* think zoos are better than the animals' natural homes. For 4, "zoos" contrasts with "fields and forests." For 5, a plural noun meaning a specific place is needed. "Residence" is inappropriate for animals.

The words tested in vocabulary problems occur 5–12 times per million; that is, for every million words used, these words will appear 5 to 12 times. Idiomatic expressions will also be tested. The test writers use the following references as guides.

John B. Carroll, et al., *The American Heritage Word Frequency Book*. New York: American Heritage Publishing, 1971.

Henry Kučera and W. Nelson Francis, *Frequency Analysis of English Usage, Lexicon, and Grammar*. Boston: Houghton Mifflin, 1982. (This is the "Brown University Corpus.")

Edward L. Thorndike and Irving Lorge, *The Teacher's Word Book of 30,000 Words*. New York: Teachers College Columbia University, 1944, 2d ed. 1952.

There are two kinds of vocabulary problems. In one kind, you will see a sentence with an underlined word or phrase. From the answer choices given below the sentence, you should choose the word or phrase that means about the same thing as the underlined word or phrase in the sentence, and which could be used in the sentence without changing its meaning. The underlined word or phrase will often be more specific, and it will occur less frequently (e.g, 5–12 times per million words) in English than the answer choices. The answer choices will be "high frequency" words that occur 50 or more times per million. You will probably know these common words. Approximately 75–80 percent of the vocabulary words are of Greco-Latin origin and about 10 percent are idiomatic expressions.

Here is an example of the first kind of vocabulary problem.

It's too windy to go for a <u>stroll</u>.
   a. swim
   b. sail
   c. drive
   d. walk

The correct answer is *d*. A "stroll" is a leisurely walk.

In the other kind of vocabulary problem, you will read a sentence with a word or phrase missing and a list of four words or phrases. You are to choose the word or phrase that best fits into the sentence in a meaningful way. Idiomatic expressions will also appear.

Here is an example of the sentence completion type of vocabulary problem:

The first things we study in school are very _____ .
   a. sturdy
   b. shifty
   c. elementary
   d. trusty

The correct answer choice is *c, elementary*. "Very" in the sentence leads you to expect an adjective, and "first things" are elementary, or basic things.

In the reading comprehension section of part 3, there are several reading passages, each followed by 3–6 questions, depending on the length of the passage. Most reading passages are about 260 words long and have 5 questions. The passages on each form of the test will cover different topics, or areas of study. Some will be in the social sciences, some natural sciences, humanities, history, medicine, etc. It is the type of reading that a university student might find in a newspaper, book, or magazine article. The reading levels, as measured by standard U.S. reading level tests, range from 11th grade (in high school) to first-year college. The questions following each passage will ask about the main idea, supporting details or facts, cause and effect relationships, the author's opinion, and drawing inferences. All the information you need to answer the questions will be in the passage; you will not need prior knowledge of the subject matter.

Several techniques can be helpful with this type of test, and you should practice them to find the method that works best for you. One method is to read the questions first, then read the passage, thinking of the questions, and then answer them. A second method is to skim through the passage for the main idea, then read the questions and reread the passage more carefully before answering the questions. A third method is to read the passage carefully, then answer the questions, looking back to the passage if necessary for details.

Here is an example of a short reading passage.

The influenza virus is a single molecule built from many millions of single atoms. Viruses are sometimes called "living molecules." While bacteria can be considered as a type of plant, secreting poisonous substances into the body of the organism they attack, viruses are living organisms themselves. We may consider them as regular chemical molecules, since they have a strictly defined atomic structure, but on the other hand we must also consider them as being alive, since they are able to multiply in unlimited quantities.

1. According to the passage, bacteria are...
   a. poisons.
   b. larger than viruses.
   c. very small.
   d. plants.

2. The writer says that viruses are alive because they...
   a. have a complex atomic structure.
   b. move.
   c. multiply.
   d. need warmth and light.

3. The atomic structure of viruses...
   a. is variable.
   b. is strictly defined.
   c. cannot be analyzed chemically.
   d. is more complex than that of bacteria.

The correct answers are 1*d*, 2*c*, 3*b*. For 1, the passage stated that "bacteria can be considered as a type of plant." For 2, you are asked *why* they are considered living. This is explained in the passage by the phrase, "*since* they are able to multiply." For 3, the passage states that viruses "have a strictly defined atomic structure."

Practice Tests

Two practice tests for part 3 follow. A sample answer sheet is in appendix E. In each practice test, there are 30 grammar, 20 cloze, 30 vocabulary, and 20 reading problems, making a total of 100 problems. The time limit for completing these 100 problems is 75 minutes (1 hour and 15 minutes). Time yourself carefully before you start, and stop when 75 minutes have passed. Following the practice tests are an answer key and commentary (pp. 100–112). Do not look at either until you have finished the test. Then, score your test, and read the commentary for the problems you missed or were uncertain about.

INSTRUCTIONS: Do not begin this part until the examiner has read these instructions with you.

1. This test contains 100 problems. There are four kinds: grammar, cloze, vocabulary, and reading comprehension. Examples of each kind of problem are given below.

2. Each problem in the test has **only one** correct answer. Make only one mark on your answer sheet for each problem. If you want to change an answer, cross out the old mark or erase it.

3. Do not make any marks in this test booklet. Write only on your answer sheet.

4. The examiner will not explain any test problem; only the examples may be explained if you do not understand the problems.

5. You will have 75 minutes to finish the entire test. Try to answer all the problems. Each problem counts the same. Do not spend too much time on any one problem or you will not have time to finish the test. Unanswered problems will be counted wrong. You may answer the problems in any order you wish.

6. Here are examples of each kind of problem. In each example, the correct answer has been marked with an asterisk (*). For the actual problems, make an X on your answer sheet inside the parentheses next to the letter of the correct answer. Do not write in this test booklet.

GRAMMAR: Choose the word or phrase that correctly completes the conversation.

> I. "What is that thing?"
> "That _____ a spider."
> a. to call
> b. for calling
> c. be called
> * d. is called

CLOZE: Read the passage, then select the word which best fills the blank in both grammar and meaning.

> Long ago roads were only trails for people
> and animals to walk on, but today roads must be made
> for cars, trucks, and buses. The most modern __(II)__   II. a. way   c. travel
> is often called a superhighway.   * b. road   d. superhighway

VOCABULARY: There are two kinds of vocabulary problems. In one kind, you must choose the word or phrase that means the same thing as the underlined word or phrase. In the other kind, you must choose the word or phrase that correctly completes the sentence.

> III. When the boat left, everyone was very joyful.
> a. sad
> b. tired
> c. angry
> * d. happy

> IV. Because of the storm and rough waves, it
> would be foolish to go out sailing today in a
> small _____.
> a. automobile
> b. house
> * c. boat
> d. beast

READING: Read the passage, then answer the questions following it according to the information given in the passage.

> While I was getting ready to go to town one morning last week, my wife handed me a
> little piece of red cloth and asked if I would have time during the day to buy her two yards of
> cloth like that.

> V. The person telling the story is . . .
> a. a married lady.
> b. an unmarried lady.
> * c. a married man.
> d. an unmarried man.

7. Fill in your name, native language, and today's date on your answer sheet. Make sure you fill in the correct form of the test in the box marked FORM at the top of your answer sheet.

8. Begin the test now. Remember, you have 75 minutes (one hour and 15 minutes) to finish the test.

Part 3, Practice Test 1

For problems 1–30, choose the word or phrase that correctly completes the sentence.

1. "In America, are most scientists well paid?"
   "Yes, the _____ are paid very well."
   a. majority of scientists
   b. majority of scientist
   c. scientists of majority
   d. scientists majority

2. "What is your job at the factory?"
   "My job is _____ all the doors at the end of the day."
   a. locking
   b. to be locking
   c. locks
   d. locked

3. "I paid $30 for a taxi from the airport last night."
   "You _____ me for a ride."
   a. would have asked
   b. could asked
   c. could ask
   d. could have asked

4. "Let's take the elevator to the 25th floor."
   "Never! Elevators are something _____ ."
   a. which I'm afraid
   b. I'm afraid of
   c. which I'm afraid of it
   d. which I'm afraid of them

5. "Why did John quit school?"
   "He told me it was because of _____ ."
   a. his failure constantly
   b. his constantly failure
   c. he failed constantly
   d. his constant failure

6. "We need more art classes."
   "I don't think so. The students _____ in art."
   a. are not interesting
   b. have not interested
   c. are not interested
   d. have not interest

7. "I can't do all this work!"
   "_____ I helped you with it?"
   a. What if
   b. That if
   c. As if
   d. However

8. "Groceries are certainly expensive."
   "Yes, each time I go shopping, I seem _____ more."
   a. spending
   b. be spending
   c. to spending
   d. to be spending

9. "The children want to play."
   "Yes, but _____ do is their homework."
   a. what should they
   b. what they should
   c. they should
   d. that should they

10. "Can you give me a receipt?"
    "Yes, that can be _____ ."
    a. easy done
    b. easy doing
    c. easily done
    d. easy to be done

11. "Did John finish his homework?"
"Yes; although he was tired, _____ it all."
a. but he did
b. despite he did
c. he did
d. that he did

12. "Do you always believe Donald?"
"Yes, I have complete trust _____ whatever he says."
a. on
b. to
c. in
d. at

13. "Why is the front door open?"
"Oh, I'm sorry. I _____ forgotten to lock it."
a. should have
b. must have
c. ought to have
d. had to have

14. "Do you like that cake?"
"Well, it has too much sugar in it, but _____ it's ok."
a. other than that
b. another of that
c. that other
d. none other than

15. "What did you think when you met Robert's mother?"
"I was very impressed _____ her friendliness."
a. on
b. of
c. by
d. at

16. "What do you want Phil for?"
"I want him _____ the house while I'm away."
a. guards
b. guarded
c. the guard of
d. guarding

17. "Why don't you paint your room blue?"
"Oh, I never thought _____ that."
a. to be done
b. of doing
c. to have done
d. to do

18. "Can you help me choose my wife a gift?"
"Certainly; first tell me _____ expensive a gift you would like to buy."
a. how
b. how much
c. as
d. as much as

19. "I took your books back to the library."
"Oh, no! I wish you _____ that."
a. didn't do
b. didn't have done
c. haven't done
d. hadn't done

20. "What's so interesting about the San Marcos River?"
"It has plant life which you can't _____ any other place."
a. find
b. find it
c. find them
d. be found

21. "Do you have any plans for the weekend?"
"I hope to _____ my house."
a. finish to paint
b. finish paint
c. finish painting
d. finishing paint

22. "Have you heard from John lately?"
"Yes, I've had news of his _____ by a famous company."
a. hire
b. been hiring
c. hired
d. being hired

23. "Is the coffee all right?"
    "It's not _____ hot enough."
    a. rather
    b. quite
    c. too
    d. fairly

24. "I hate cooked carrots."
    "Would you like _____ raw?"
    a. as
    b. they are
    c. to be
    d. them

25. "What do you dislike about that store?"
    "Other _____ their high prices, nothing."
    a. than
    b. from
    c. except
    d. besides

26. "Dr. Jones wants to see you in his office immediately."
    "Why _____ see him?"
    a. must I
    b. I must
    c. have I to
    d. I have to

27. "Let's ask Hugh if we can use his car."
    "Willy's car is easier to _____ ."
    a. starts
    b. start
    c. be started
    d. be starting

28. "Isn't little Millicent charming!"
    "Yes, I have never seen _____ child."
    a. a so lovely
    b. such lovely a
    c. so lovely a
    d. a such lovely

29. "What do you think of this apartment?"
    "Oh, it's very expensive; _____ it's much larger than what I really want."
    a. even so
    b. moreover
    c. in spite of
    d. although

30. "Do you come here often?"
    "No. In fact, _____ ."
    a. hardly ever
    b. ever hardly
    c. never hardly
    d. hardly never

For problems 31–50, choose the word that best fits each blank both in grammar and in meaning.

An American climatologist has found evidence that five major shifts in the climate of the northern hemisphere over the last 12,000 years may have led to profound cultural changes. His conclusions are based on a __(31)__ of the records from some 470 __(32)__ and the geological evidence for when __(33)__ changes occurred. Scientists have long known (34) every few hundred years, earth's prevailing __(35)__ has undergone dramatic changes within a __(36)__ of only a few years. All __(37)__ become generally cooler or warmer; annual __(38)__ rises or falls significantly. Sea level __(39)__ or falls. The last such change __(40)__ about 800 years ago. England __(41)__ Europe became cooler and more moist __(42)__ they had been for 300 years, __(43)__ in North America, the climate became __(44)__ and cooler. All over the northern __(45)__ the climates changed. The reason is __(46)__ to have been a massive, global __(47)__ in the wind patterns of the __(48)__ atmosphere. Major climatic conditions are governed __(49)__ such winds which, every few centuries, __(50)__ their direction. Nobody knows for sure why this happens.

31. a. statistic   c. comparison
    b. result   d. data

32. a. evidence   c. scientific
    b. data   d. cultures

33. a. change   c. this
    b. climatic   d. do

34. a. that   c. in
    b. changes   d. it

35. a. climate   c. variation
    b. which   d. change

36. a. pattern   c. period
    b. notice   d. lot

37. a. shifts   c. seasons
    b. changes   d. earth

38. a. weather   c. rainfall
    b. sun   d. crop

39. a. increase   c. ups
    b. high   d. rises

40. a. took   c. in
    b. takes   d. was

41. a. and   c. not
    b. in   d. but

42. a. than   c. how
    b. climate   d. as

43. a. Canada   c. somewhere
    b. while   d. even

44. a. drier   c. humidity
    b. warmer   d. less

45. a. have   c. hemisphere
    b. did   d. all

46. a. that   c. due
    b. going   d. believed

47. a. rotates   c. air
    b. climate   d. shift

48. a. above   c. upper
    b. climate   d. windy

49. a. mostly   c. in
    b. by   d. for

50. a. change   c. turn
    b. especially   d. in

For problems 51–65, choose the word or phrase that means the same thing as the underlined word or phrase.

51. Peter was <u>positive</u> he would see Fred.
    a. certain
    b. afraid
    c. surprised
    d. happy

52. He <u>trailed</u> me.
    a. answered
    b. found
    c. followed
    d. carried

53. He <u>grabbed</u> my book.
    a. talked about
    b. suddenly took
    c. lost
    d. returned

54. The dog <u>trembled</u> when it saw the bone.
    a. shook
    b. begged
    c. barked
    d. jumped

55. The farmers <u>encountered</u> a group of soldiers.
    a. fought
    b. helped
    c. fed
    d. met

56. His remarks about the economy <u>baffled</u> me.
    a. confused
    b. relieved
    c. worried
    d. interested

57. She did not know why she felt so <u>despondent.</u>
    a. hopeless
    b. bored
    c. happy
    d. excited

58. He told me it was <u>a snap.</u>
    a. difficult
    b. good
    c. easy
    d. bad

59. Edward made a <u>feeble</u> reply.
    a. calm
    b. weak
    c. sincere
    d. slow

60. He's not a very <u>credible</u> lecturer.
    a. well-known
    b. religious
    c. ordinary
    d. believable

61. He <u>contemplated</u> becoming a jet pilot.
    a. preferred
    b. suggested
    c. considered
    d. tried

62. She <u>shoved</u> him.
    a. pushed
    b. watched
    c. called
    d. reminded

63. Oscar did the job <u>grudgingly.</u>
    a. immediately
    b. unwillingly
    c. easily
    d. carefully

64. He thinks that method is <u>prevalent.</u>
    a. advanced
    b. common
    c. difficult
    d. old-fashioned

65. He was only <u>speculating</u> about the cost.
    a. worrying
    b. complaining
    c. asking
    d. guessing

For problems 66–80, choose the word or phrase that correctly completes the sentence.

66. Tim doesn't know anything about literature and he is just as _____ of biology.
    a. partial
    b. ignorant
    c. approximate
    d. abbreviated

67. I think that bridge can hold this truck; it looks very _____ to me.
    a. muscular
    b. sturdy
    c. noble
    d. elaborate

68. The city tried to stop crime by hiring more police, but that _____ did not work.
    a. approach
    b. application
    c. management
    d. version

69. John wrote home to say he liked school. But his parents knew he was homesick because they _____ .
    a. called him to account
    b. begged the question
    c. marked his words
    d. read between the lines

70. It is very difficult to understand Roger because he _____ whenever he speaks.
    a. muffles
    b. dims
    c. sprinkles
    d. mutters

71. Alex isn't very friendly; he keeps a _____ between himself and other people.
    a. gauge
    b. foundation
    c. frontier
    d. barrier

72. There are many good bakeries in Milltown; in fact, the baking industry is _____ .
    a. adhesive
    b. flourishing
    c. incidental
    d. accommodating

73. Don't water the new seeds too much; just _____ them.
    a. sprinkle
    b. trigger
    c. wrinkle
    d. filter

74. Francis didn't have to do anything to get the money; it was _____ gift.
    a. an outright
    b. a predominant
    c. a retentive
    d. a saturated

75. For many years, they have _____ an office in that building.
    a. persisted
    b. remained
    c. maintained
    d. withheld

76. His friendliness and helpfulness are _____ that make everyone like him.
    a. principles
    b. attributes
    c. functions
    d. regimens

77. Lucy delayed the bus because she was _____ in her purse for the correct change.
    a. baffling
    b. stuffing
    c. lurching
    d. fumbling

78. Arnold couldn't decide and _____ for several minutes before acting.
    a. hesitated
    b. alternated
    c. suspended
    d. apprehended

79. While the main army attacked from the east, a small group of soldiers made a _____ in the north.
    a. diffraction
    b. dismissal
    c. diversion
    d. deterrent

80. After his heart attack he had to stop playing football, tennis, and other _____ sports.
    a. precarious
    b. strenuous
    c. ardent
    d. compressed

For problems 81–100, read the passages, then answer the questions following them according to the information given in the passage.

Sponges are just barely animals, such a borderline case that until the 19th century they were called zoophytes, the animal-plants. They are among the most primitive forms of multi-cellular animal life; they have no muscles or nerves, no mouth or digestive cavity, nothing in the way of organs. But they have been around a long time and must be doing something right. More than 5,000 species inhabit this planet, living in fresh water and throughout the sea down to depths of more than 25,000 feet.

Often strikingly beautiful, sponges offer the added virtue of usefulness. Even with synthetic sponges widely available, a market for natural sponges persists. They hold more water without dripping, are easier to clean, and last longer, even under heavy use. And now, after centuries in the bathtub, sponges are finding their way into the laboratories of pharmacologists and cell biologists. As do so many marine invertebrates that have limited defenses in the usual sense (they are capable of neither fight nor flight), sponges produce some extremely powerful chemical compounds, toxic and otherwise, that hold great promise as future drugs for the treatment of human disorders, including cancer.

81. According to the passage, why are sponges of interest to pharmacologists and biologists?
    a. because of their digestive system
    b. because of the chemicals they produce
    c. because they are neither plant nor animal
    d. because they are primitive

82. The author says that sponges are "doing something right" because they . . .
    a. are strikingly beautiful.
    b. are preferred over synthetics.
    c. might be used against cancer.
    d. have existed for centuries.

83. The author mentions the lack of mouth and digestive cavity of sponges to show that sponges . . .
    a. are primitive.
    b. are multicellular.
    c. are animals.
    d. are zoophytes.

84. One can infer from the passage that the traditional use for sponges was to use them . . .
    a. for bathing.
    b. for medicine.
    c. for decoration.
    d. for laboratory study.

85. According to the passage, before the 19th century, sponges were erroneously believed to be . . .
    a. just barely animals.
    b. both plant and animal.
    c. both vertebrate and invertebrate.
    d. single–celled.

Until recently, because of the difficulty of testing hearing in small children, deafness often wasn't detected until a child was about two, too late to prevent a permanent language handicap. Now, however, there is a method to test infants' hearing by measuring electrical activity generated by the brain stem in response to sound. Through earphones, an infant is presented with a series of clicking sounds that stimulate the auditory nervous system. The electrical activity thus evoked in the brain is in turn picked up by electrodes placed behind each ear. These electrical signals are amplified, fed into a computer and printed out as waves on a graph. Within 12.5 milliseconds of a click, the graph of a normal baby will show seven distinct peaks, each representing a point along the path the sound has taken from the auditory nerve to the hearing centers of the cortex. For a baby with impaired hearing, the peaks take longer to appear. Different types of hearing defects, moreover, will produce wave patterns that deviate from the normal in characteristic ways. For example, absence of all seven waves indicates total sensory-neural deafness, usually untreatable. In conductive deafness, which can be treated, wave patterns will emerge if the intensity of the sound is increased.

86. The graph suggests that an infant's hearing problem can be helped if . . .
    a. no peaks appear on the graph.
    b. the waves are longer than the waves of normal infants.
    c. waves appear in less than 12.5 milliseconds of a click.
    d. waves only appear when the clicking sounds are made louder.

87. What is the function of the electrodes mentioned in the paragraph?
    a. They transmit the clicks to the computer.
    b. They detect the clicking sounds.
    c. They detect electrical activity in the brain.
    d. They stimulate the auditory nervous system.

88. What test results occur when an infant's hearing problem cannot be helped?
    a. No waves appear on the graph.
    b. The wave patterns are longer than those of a normal infant.
    c. The peaks on the graph are irregularly spaced.
    d. Peaks appear only when the intensity of the sound increases.

89. What is the function of the computer in this test?
    a. It sends electrical signals through the earphones.
    b. It transforms electrical signals into a printed pattern.
    c. It transforms electrical signals into sounds.
    d. It amplifies electrical signals.

90. According to the passage, why is this hearing test such an important development?
    a. It is more accurate than any other hearing test.
    b. It can be used on babies.
    c. It is not difficult to learn to administer the test.
    d. It is not difficult to learn to interpret the test.

Many 19th-century illusionists brought to their profession a zestful appetite for science. Most were grounded in ancient varieties of sleight of hand, and combined them with such specialities as juggling, ventriloquism, or mind reading. But they also found, in that century of prolific invention, that every new scientific invention had magic possibilities. The magician made it his business to stay a step or two ahead of public understanding of science.

The magic lantern had been used for private entertainment by the well-to-do in the 17th century, but late in the 18th century it suddenly acquired a virtuoso role in public entertainment. The genius behind this development was a Belgian experimenter, Etienne Robert. In 1797, when he acquired an abandoned chapel, surrounded by ancient tombs, on the grounds of an old Parisian monastery, he scored a historic success. Audiences entered through cavernous corridors, marked with strange symbols, and came on a dimly lit chamber decorated with skulls; effects of thunder, sepulchral music, and tolling bells helped to set the mood. Coal burned in braziers. Robert gave a preliminary discourse, denouncing charlatans and their bogus apparitions and promising something superior. He tossed some chemicals on the braziers, causing columns of smoke to rise. The single lamp flickered out, putting the audience in almost total darkness. Then, onto the smoke arising from the braziers, images were projected from his concealed magic lanterns. They included human forms and unearthly spectral shapes. The images came from glass slides, but the movements of the smoke gave them a ghoulish kind of life. Some spectators sank to their knees, convinced they were in the presence of the supernatural.

91. The main idea of this passage is that . . .
    a. magic can be used to explain scientific principles.
    b. magicians used advanced scientific knowledge to produce "magic."
    c. magic shows were very popular in the 17th century.
    d. magic is beyond the comprehension of the ordinary person.

92. According to the author, what did 19th-century magicians combine to produce their magic effects?
    a. mysterious sights and sounds
    b. mind reading and the supernatural
    c. superior intelligence and a gullible public
    d. skills and scientific knowledge

93. What made the images mentioned in the passage move?
    a. The glass slides moved back and forth.
    b. The magic lantern moved back and forth.
    c. They were projected onto moving smoke.
    d. They changed as the film moved through the projector.

94. How did Robert use the magic lantern?
    a. to decorate the chamber
    b. to project images
    c. to burn the chemicals
    d. to provide light in the room

95. The author uses Etienne Robert in this passage as an example of . . .
    a. a charlatan who used bogus apparitions.
    b. a gifted controller of the supernatural.
    c. an unrecognized scientific genius.
    d. a magician who used popularly unknown scientific techniques.

Some people dry mushrooms for winter use, and some can them. From my experience, I've found that freezing them produces erratic results: some species freeze well, while others do not. This is an area for experimentation on the part of each collector. Generally speaking, those forms like the brick cap, which fruit late in the fall, preserve fairly well by the deep-freeze technique.

Drying mushrooms, however, is one of the best ways of preserving them. Good circulation of warm air around the actual pieces being dried is the most important principle to be remembered here. But the specimens should not be overheated to the point that the tissue collapses and becomes wet. Since overheating almost always takes place if drying is done in an oven, the preferred method is to use a set of screens arranged one above the other. A sheet of flame-proofed canvas should be wrapped around it to obtain the effect of a chimney, and a hot plate placed at the bottom and used to provide steady heat. Steady heat is a cardinal point, since if the specimens are allowed to cool off when partly dried they become soggy and are not as good when finally dried out completely. When the pieces of mushroom on the screens have become crisp, they should be removed and stored in moisture-proof and insect-proof glass jars. To save space, only carefully cleaned, solid young mushrooms should be dried. As dried mushrooms mold very readily under conditions of high humidity and can become infested with the larvae of small beetles, the above-mentioned precautions are very important.

96. According to the author, what happens if the source of heat isn't constant?
    a. The mushrooms don't dry thoroughly.
    b. The mushrooms become overheated.
    c. The mushrooms expand and waste space.
    d. The mushrooms become insect-infested.

97. What does the author say about freezing mushrooms?
    a. Freezing preserves all mushrooms fairly well.
    b. Freezing is the best way to keep mold from spoiling the mushrooms.
    c. Freezing works well for only certain types of mushrooms.
    d. Freezing is the best way to take the moisture out of mushrooms.

98. The author uses the brick cap as an example of . . .
    a. a deep-freeze technique.
    b. a collector's experiment.
    c. a late-fruiting mushroom.
    d. a mushroom preserver.

99. What can be done to protect dried mushrooms from mold and larvae?
    a. Mushrooms must be stored in moisture- and insect-proof glass jars.
    b. Only solid, young, carefully cleaned mushrooms must be used.
    c. Steady heat must be maintained when drying the mushrooms.
    d. The mushrooms must be dried very carefully and completely.

100. According to the author, the most important part in the drying procedure is . . .
    a. putting the mushrooms in a hot oven.
    b. circulation of warm air around the mushrooms.
    c. cooling the mushrooms at the right time.
    d. storing the mushrooms in moisture- and insect-proof jars.

End Practice Test 1.

Part 3: Grammar, Cloze, Vocabulary, Reading

INSTRUCTIONS: Do not begin this part until the examiner has read these instructions with you.

1. This test contains 100 problems. There are four kinds: grammar, cloze, vocabulary, and reading comprehension. Examples of each kind of problem are given below.

2. Each problem in the test has only one correct answer. Make only one mark on your answer sheet for each problem. If you want to change an answer, cross out the old mark or erase it.

3. Do not make any marks in this test booklet. Write only on your answer sheet.

4. The examiner will not explain any test problem; only the examples may be explained if you do not understand the problems.

5. You will have 75 minutes to finish the entire test. Try to answer all the problems. Each problem counts the same. Do not spend too much time on any one problem or you will not have time to finish the test. Unanswered problems will be counted wrong. You may answer the problems in any order you wish.

6. Here are examples of each kind of problem. In each example, the correct answer has been marked with an asterisk (*). For the actual problems, make an X on your answer sheet inside the parentheses next to the letter of the correct answer. Do not write in this test booklet.

GRAMMAR: Choose the word or phrase that correctly completes the conversation.

I. "What is that thing?"
"That _____ a spider."
    a. to call
    b. for calling
    c. be called
  * d. is called

CLOZE: Read the passage, then select the word which best fills the blank in both grammar and meaning.

Long ago roads were only trails for people and animals to walk on, but today roads must be made for cars, trucks, and buses. The most modern (II) is often called a superhighway.

II. a. way   c. travel
 * b. road   d. superhighway

VOCABULARY: There are two kinds of vocabulary problems. In one kind, you must choose the word or phrase that means the same thing as the underlined word or phrase. In the other kind, you must choose the word or phrase that correctly completes the sentence.

III. When the boat left, everyone was very joyful.
    a. sad
    b. tired
    c. angry
  * d. happy

IV. Because of the storm and rough waves, it would be foolish to go out sailing today in a small _____.
    a. automobile
    b. house
  * c. boat
    d. beast

READING: Read the passage, then answer the questions following it according to the information given in the passage.

While I was getting ready to go to town one morning last week, my wife handed me a little piece of red cloth and asked if I would have time during the day to buy her two yards of cloth like that.

V. The person telling the story is . . .
    a. a married lady.
    b. an unmarried lady.
  * c. a married man.
    d. an unmarried man.

7. Fill in your name, native language, and today's date on your answer sheet. Make sure you fill in the correct form of the test in the box marked FORM at the top of your answer sheet.

8. Begin the test now. Remember, you have 75 minutes (one hour and 15 minutes) to finish the test.

Part 3, Practice Test 2

For problems 1–30, choose the word or phrase that best fits into the sentence.

1. "Have you ever been to Hawaii?"
   "No, but I've thought about _____ there."
   a. going
   b. go
   c. to go
   d. will go

2. "Do you mind if people use your car?"
   "Not really, but it _____ that I'm getting tired of it."
   a. so often happens
   b. too often happens
   c. happens so often
   d. happens too often

3. "Can you meet me for lunch today?"
   "Yes, I _____ time to finish my housework by noon."
   a. will be having
   b. have had
   c. had
   d. will have had

4. "Professor Smith is very young."
   "Perhaps that is true, but she is _____ the most intelligent teacher in the university."
   a. moreover
   b. too
   c. even
   d. nonetheless

5. "Were you able to save anything from the fire?"
   "No, it happened so fast _____ anything we could do."
   a. that wasn't
   b. there wasn't
   c. wasn't
   d. it wasn't

6. "Do you eat in restaurants often?"
   "Not _____ I used to."
   a. as much as
   b. so much
   c. so much that
   d. as much

7. "Where should I put this dirty shirt?"
   "The clothing _____ is next to the washing machine."
   a. to be laundered
   b. for laundered
   c. laundering
   d. of laundering

8. "Do I have to apply for a new library card every year?"
   "No, your card is good for a _____ period."
   a. two years
   b. two year
   c. of two years
   d. two of years

9. "I thought the convention was always in March."
   "Usually it is, but next year it _____ in April."
   a. will hold
   b. is held
   c. will being holding
   d. is being held

10. "Did Betty and Donna sell many tickets?"
    "Yes, _____ the two of them, they sold nearly 100."
    a. besides
    b. by
    c. between
    d. for

11. "Was the concert held last night?"
"No, it was called _____ because of the storm."
a. off
b. down
c. out
d. over

12. "The store manager called about your order."
"When _____ shipped?"
a. did he say was it
b. he said it was
c. did he say it was
d. it was he did say

13. "Are typing and shorthand required for the job?"
"Yes, those and _____ skills are necessary."
b. other
a. others
c. another
d. anothers

14. "Why aren't you washing the clothes?"
"All the soap _____ up two days ago."
a. was used
b. has used
c. have used
d. used

15. "How was summer school?"
"I took several interesting courses _____ ."
a. which were also useful
b. of which were useful too
c. and as well useful
d. and useful too

16. "How long will the potatoes take?"
"They should _____ for at least an hour."
a. baked
b. bakes
c. be bake
d. bake

17. "You seem bored."
"I am. I've done _____ sit around the house all day."
a. nothing than
b. nothing but
c. none else but
d. not else but

18. "Are Karen and Sue good friends?"
"Yes, they _____ each other for years."
a. have been knowing
b. are knowing
c. have known
d. know

19. "Joe was told to leave the party."
"I'm not surprised. His rude behavior wasn't _____ ."
a. suitable
b. suiting
c. suited
d. suitably

20. "Why is John so late?"
"He had _____ a phone call."
a. stopping to make
b. to stop making
c. to stop to make
d. stopping making

21. "Do you need any help?"
"No, I want to do this myself, and not let somebody else _____ for me."
a. do it
b. to do
c. to do it
d. do

22. "Do you know that girl?"
"Yes, but I can't remember _____ ."
a. from where do I know her
b. where do I know her from
c. where from I know her
d. where I know her from

23. "What musical instruments do you play?"
    "I studied violin as a child, but now I _____ almost everything."
    a. am forgetting
    b/ have forgotten
    c. do forget
    d. forget

24. "Did you hear that David got a video recorder?"
    "No. _____ , we would have come right over."
    a/ Had we known
    b. Were we known
    c. If we know
    d. Did we know

25. "Coffee is bad for your body."
    "Yes, I really must stop _____ it every day."
    a/ drinking
    b. to drink
    c. drink
    d. drunk

26. "Did you hear his plan?"
    "Yes, _____ clever ideas he has."
    a. which
    b. that
    c. how
    d/ what

27. "Is it hard to build a birdhouse?"
    "That depends on who is _____ ."
    a. doing the build
    b/ doing the building
    c. done the building
    d. done the build

28. "Do you have any red pencils?"
    "No, they're _____ black."
    a. some
    b. scarcely
    c/ mostly
    d. a few

29. "Please come to visit me tonight."
    "OK, I'll stop by your house, _____ it's late."
    a. even so
    b. even
    c. even that
    d/ even if

30. "That's not the best way to do that."
    "How else _____ ?"
    a. can it be doing
    b. it can be done
    c. it can be doing
    d/ can it be done

Drugs, despite their seemingly magical contributions to human health and comfort, have always been a mixed blessing. They have a capacity for great __(31)__ as well as great benefit; they __(32)__ be formulated and used carefully __(33)__ knowledgeably. Modern pharmaceutical scientists stress the need __(34)__ unremitting research to take the magic—and __(35)__ the uncertainty—out of the action __(36)__ drugs. One of their major __(37)__ is how to formulate a drug __(38)__ that it will work at the __(39)__ speed at the proper site in __(40)__ body without harming the patient in __(41)__ way.

Several researchers at the University of Michigan have been working on this __(42)__, and closely related questions, for several __(43)__ and within the framework of a __(44)__ of long term projects. Their basic __(45)__ is to find the best dosage __(46)__ any given drug and to be __(47)__ to predict its activity so precisely __(48)__ the proper regimen can be prescribed __(49)__ achieve optimal positive and __(50)__ negative effects. In this way, the accumulated knowledge of the pharmaceutical scientist serves as a tool for the physician.

31. a. loss   c. advantage
     b. care   d. harm

32. a. could   c. would
     b. must   d. used

33. a. and   c. also
     b. with   d. very

34. a. to   c. for
     b. and   d. in

35. a. harm   c. thus
     b. use   d. not

36. a. of   c. toward
     b. from   d. any

37. a. discoveries   c. concerns
     b. abilities   d. actions

38. a. beneficial   c. composition
     b. besides   d. so

39. a. most   c. high
     b. rate   d. best

40. a. the   c. sick
     b. human   d. patient

41. a. other   c. several
     b. wrong   d. any

42. a. problem   c. field
     b. respect   d. theory

43. a. times   c. fields
     b. years   d. without

44. a. success   c. variety
     b. work   d. problem

45. a. foundation   c. item
     b. goal   d. look

46. a. to   c. than
     b. for   d. against

47. a. used   c. made
     b. tested   d. able

48. a. that   c. why
     b. as   d. and

49. a. as   c. that
     b. to   d. for

50. a. positive   c. also
     b. optimal   d. minimal

For problems 51–65, choose the word or phrase that means the same thing as the underlined word or phrase.

51. What is the significance of the king's visit?
    a. cause
    b. probability
    c. danger
    d, importance

52. He was fuming when we came in.
    a. smiling
    b. thinking
    c/ angry
    d. smoking

53. That will require some deliberation.
    a, thought
    b. action
    c. help
    d. attention

54. I don't know what John is driving at.
    a. tried
    b, means
    c. became
    d. thinks

55. The group solicited our support.
    a. refused
    b. appreciated
    c. mentioned
    d, requested

56. People say that John Smith is very eccentric.
    a. proud
    b. neat
    c, odd
    d. nervous

57. We were appalled by his actions.
    a. amused
    b, shocked
    c. confused
    d. saved

58. Everyone got in the brawl.
    a. game
    b. conversation
    c. committee
    d., fight

59. The tugboat escorted the battleship.
    a. chased
    b, guided
    c. passed
    d. followed

60. Bob didn't have an alibi.
    a, an excuse
    b. a speech
    c. a solution
    d. a report

61. My new roommate is quite amiable.
    a, pleasant
    b. serious
    c. shy
    d. lively

62. Tom Whittle was foremost in his field.
    a. a builder
    b. an officer
    c, a leader
    d. a beginner

63. His assertion angered us.
    a, statement
    b. question
    c. success
    d. mistake

64. They compiled the information for us.
    a. studied
    b, gathered
    c. kept
    d. mixed

65. Have you met the eminent Dr. Connors?
    a/ famous
    b. wise
    c. successful
    d. wealthy

For problems 66–80, choose the word or phrase that correctly completes the sentence.

66. The loose powder was _____ into a small container.
    a. compressed
    b. descended
    c. intensified
    d. resolved

67. Many apples are grown every year in that large _____ over there.
    a. provision
    b. cultivation
    c. harvest
    d. orchard

68. Be careful; this patient's disease is _____ .
    a. congenial
    b. accessible
    c. compulsory
    d. contagious

69. The hot, dry weather caused the tomato plants to _____ .
    a. stifle
    b. shutter
    c. wither
    d. crouch

70. Beth gave half of the money to her parents, but she kept the _____ .
    a. remainder
    b. overthrow
    c. particle
    d. remnant

71. This book isn't printed clearly; everything is _____ .
    a. biased
    b. blurred
    c. giddy
    d. filtered

72. At first, Charles said he'd never move to Alaska, but now he seems _____ to the idea.
    a. narrowed
    b. destined
    c. resigned
    d. indulged

73. The accident happened because the driver was blinded by the _____ of the setting sun.
    a. gaze
    b. streak
    c. glare
    d. splash

74. I didn't like the way the job was being done, so I used an _____ approach.
    a. alternative
    b. auxiliary
    c. approximate
    d. ambiguous

75. He cut his feet climbing up on the sharp, _____ rocks.
    a. stuffed
    b. jagged
    c. limp
    d. grizzly

76. Because we will never agree about this, any further discussion is _____ .
    a. discernible
    b. heedless
    c. futile
    d. reflective

77. Harold came to the _____ that Larry had lied.
    a. standpoint
    b. outcome
    c. result
    d. conclusion

78. Susan and Jane had to share the prize because they finished the race _____ .
    a. overwhelmingly
    b. simultaneously
    c. profoundly
    d. exclusively

79. Although I disagree with Joan, I try to be _____ of her opinions.
    a. animated towards
    b. tolerant of
    c. resigned to
    d. callous about

80. She said he hadn't arrived yet, but that she expected him _____ .
    a. momentously
    b. monumentally
    c. minutely
    d. momentarily

The record of people's manipulation of nature in the Florida Everglades is replete with examples of remedies that were never fully analyzed before they were applied—remedies that inevitably turned out to be more disastrous than the troubles they were intended to cure. It was people's judgment, for example, that the rich muck of South Florida was going to waste under water; so people drained off the water only to discover that muck, exposed to the heat of the sun, oxidizes into thin air. In some agricultural districts now as much as 40 percent of the organic soils are gone. Some farmers will be ploughing limestone by the year 2000. But they won't be raising any crops. Similarly, drainage undertaken to increase food production in one area has inhibited productivity in another; in periods of drought, the long canals became arms of the sea and salt water intruded on the land. In 1945, salinity in the soil killed off 18,000 acres of vegetables in southeast Dade county. Now increasing salinity in Florida Bay, caused by the decreasing outflow of fresh water from the Everglades, threatens the natural offshore nursery ground of the Tortugas shrimp and a $20 million annual commercial fishery.

81. One can infer from the passage that the canals were constructed in order to . . .
   a. reduce the danger of flooding.
   b. improve transportation.
   c/ increase crop productivity.
   d. provide an entrance to the sea.

82. According to the passage, the canals allowed . . .
   a. the limestone to be exposed to air.
   b. seawater to drain from the land.
   c/ seawater to enter farmlands.
   d. the prevention of floods.

83. According to the passage, what do Tortugas shrimp require in their nurseries?
   a/ some fresh water mixed with the salt water
   b. a heavy concentration of salt water
   c. rapidly moving water
   d. a high, steady water temperature

84. Seawater is found in the canals when . . .
   a./ there is a dry spell.
   b. there is a flood.
   c. the fresh water is diverted elsewhere.
   d. the organic soils are gone.

85. Why was the water drained off the muck?
   a. to reduce the salinity in the soil
   b. so the muck would oxidize
   c. so the water could be used
   d/ so the muck could be used

The worldwide consumption of bakery products is increasing. Many populations that formerly relied solely on rice or coarser grains as their main source of carbohydrates show a preference for compounded bakery products as new industry and increased incomes make them more widely accessible. Japan is an outstanding example of countries following this trend. The United States has shown a steady downward trend in per capita consumption of cereal-based foods for many years, and the consumption of sweet bakery foods, such as cakes or pastry, has been increasingly displacing bread consumption.

Probably 95% of the white bread sold in the United States is enriched with thiamine, niacin, riboflavin, and iron, and about 30 of the 50 states have laws requiring white bread enrichment. Formerly, calcium and vitamin D were frequently added to enriched bread, but lack of consumer demand and questionable nutritional benefit led to gradual phasing out of these enrichments. India has attempted to encourage consumption of protein-enriched bread, with some success. Except for research projects, little has been done in other countries, however. In areas where bakery products comprise a large proportion of the diet, they could provide an ideal vehicle for nutritional supplementation. The need for better quality protein in the daily diet occurs mostly in the developing countries, where carbohydrate foods—usually cereals—are the basic components of the diet and therefore the logical protein carriers.

86. The main idea of the passage is that there is a worldwide trend towards . . .
   a. enriching the nutritional value of bread.
   b. using grains, such as rice, as a source of carbohydrates.
   c. increasing the consumption of protein.
   d. using bakery products as a source of carbohydrates.

87. According to the passage, in developing countries where there is heavy consumption of carbohydrate foods . . .
   a. protein enrichment of bread is not needed to supplement the diet.
   b. calcium and vitamin D are often added to supplement the diet.
   c. laws requiring white bread enrichment are needed.
   d. carbohydrate foods are ideal carriers for nutritional supplements.

88. Because of little demand and questionable value . . .
   a. calcium and vitamin D are no longer added to bread.
   b. cereal-based foods are being replaced by bakery products.
   c. little has been done to encourage consumption of enriched bread.
   d. rice and coarser grains are being replaced by bakery products.

89. Japan is used in this passage to illustrate a trend in many countries . . .
   a. to increase a reliance on rice and grains.
   b. to increase consumption of bakery foods.
   c. to enrich bread.
   d. to make industry more accessible.

90. In developing countries, popular cereals could be the best way to . . .
   a. increase reliance on carbohydrates.
   b. supplement the diet.
   c. encourage research projects.
   d. phase out necessary bread enrichments.

One of medicine's fundamental beliefs about pregnancy and the development of the human fetus has been challenged. Until recently, it was thought that the fetus was a parasite capable of extracting all the nutrients it needed from the mother. It is now realized that adequate nutrition during the entire course of the pregnancy is necessary for proper fetal development.

In early pregnancy, certain changes occur in the mother's gastrointestinal tract, resulting in more efficient absorption of specific nutrients, such as iron and calcium. Furthermore, the maternal blood supply increases, so that nutrients can be transported via the uterine and placental blood systems. If the mother is undernourished, this "lifeline" to the fetus will be inadequately developed. Finally, fat is accumulated within the body to store the energy necessary for lactation (milk production). This preparation for lactation is so important that if the mother is inadequately nourished, it will take place even at the expense of fetal growth. It is a logical developmental occurrence, since in the natural world, no infant can survive without successful breastfeeding, and thus fetal growth is less of a priority.

91. The main point of the passage is a discussion of . . .
    a. how the human fetus develops.
    b. methods of achieving proper maternal nutrition.
    c. the benefits of breastfeeding.
    d. the effect of maternal nutrition on the fetus.

92. What is required for lactation?
    a. increased blood supply
    b. iron and calcium
    c. fat storage
    d. a well-nourished placenta

93. What is the "lifeline" mentioned in the passage?
    a. the gastrointestinal tract
    b. breastfeeding
    c. accumulated fat
    d. uterine and placental blood systems

94. What takes precedence over fetal growth?
    a. preparation for lactation
    b. fetal fat accumulation
    c. successful breastfeeding
    d. parasitic capabilities of the fetus

95. According to the passage, what traditional belief has been questioned?
    a. The fetus grows at the expense of the mother.
    b. Good nutrition is necessary throughout pregnancy.
    c. The mother's nourishment is more important than the baby's.
    d. The most important changes occur in early pregnancy.

Monticello ("little mountain") in Virginia is the estate and residence once owned by Thomas Jefferson, third president of the United States. Jefferson inherited the property in 1757 on the death of his father, Peter Jefferson, who in 1735 was given a government grant for this 1000 acre tract south of the Rivanna River, and who had subsequently acquired from a friend 400 additional acres for a homesite north of the Rivanna. Jefferson began having the mountaintop leveled for his homesite in 1768. There being no competent architect in the colonies to carry out his instructions, he mastered architecture by the study of books and drew his own plans, deriving his principal inspiration from the works of the Italian architect Andrea Palladio (1518-1580). Begun in 1769, the residence was developed in intermittent stages as its busy master found opportunity to return to it from his wanderings on the political and diplomatic scene, and it did not reach completion until after he left the presidency in 1809. He began occupying it in February 1770, after his paternal home at Shadwell, north of the Rivanna, had been destroyed by fire. The entire residence is one of the finest examples of the classical revival style, of which Jefferson was the first exponent in America.

96. Why did Thomas Jefferson study architecture?
   a. He wanted to help the architect design Monticello.
   b. He couldn't find an architect capable of designing his house.
   c. His father wanted him to study it.
   d. He wished to improve the buildings at Shadwell.

97. According to the passage, the original house at Shadwell was . . .
   a. designed by Peter Jefferson.
   b. built in the classical revival style.
   c. destroyed by fire, then rebuilt.
   d. the home of Peter Jefferson.

98. Why did it take as long as it did to build the residence at Monticello?
   a. Thomas Jefferson was busy elsewhere.
   b. It was destroyed by fire during its construction.
   c. It wasn't necessary to hurry, as Shadwell was available as a residence.
   d. It took that long for Thomas Jefferson to master architecture.

99. Why is Thomas Jefferson associated with the classical revival style?
   a. He admired and advocated it.
   b. His buildings are the only examples of it in the U.S.
   c. He tried to replace it with a more purely American style.
   d. He popularized it after his father invented it.

100. Why did Thomas Jefferson move into Monticello when he did?
   a. It was finally completed.
   b. He finally retired from the presidency.
   c. The house at Shadwell burned down.
   d. His father died, leaving him the estate.

End Practice Test 2.

Part 4: Oral Interview (Optional)

The oral interview is not automatically included in every MELAB administration, but it is required for candidates sponsored by WHO, IMF, and GMI, and for state nursing boards and University of Michigan applicants. If you are applying at the graduate level to a university in the United States and want to be considered for a teaching assistantship in order to get financial aid, it is strongly recommended that you include the oral interview in your MELAB test. There is an additional fee for the interview.

You will have a 10 to 15 minute conversation with the local examiner, who will rate you on your fluency in spoken English, your grammar and vocabulary range and accuracy, your pronunciation, and your understanding of spoken English. Your ability to make your meaning clear and to respond appropriately will be considered.

The examiner will ask you questions about your background and your future plans, and your opinions on certain issues. The examiner might ask you to explain or describe in detail something about your field or specialization. For example:

What schools have you applied to in the United States?
How did you happen to choose that school?
What do you plan to study there?
How long does a master's degree program in (your field) take?
Have you had any personal contact with any of your future professors?
What exactly does a (mechanical engineer/art historian) do?
What changes have occurred in your field over the last 25 years?
How does the work of a (dentist/architect/electrical engineer) of today differ from one of 25 years ago?
What are your long-range plans? What do you plan to do after you finish your degree?

You should try to give more than a simple "yes" or "no" answer to the examiner's questions. If you do not understand a question, do not be afraid to ask the examiner to repeat or rephrase it.

It is common to be nervous in oral interviews. The examiner knows this and will try to make you relaxed, so that you can do your best.

Possible scores for the oral interview are 4, 3, 2, and 1, with 4 being the highest. If the examiner thinks your spoken English is good for your level, but not strong enough to raise it to the next level, s/he may add a plus (+) to your score, for example: 3+. The average oral rating is 2+.

Here are some brief descriptions of the kind of language seen at each level.

4: Fluency and command of English similar to a native speaker. Occasional deviations in grammar, lexis, or pronunciation do not cause miscommunication. Is able to use both formal and colloquial English; is able to use terms specific to his/her field of study effectively.

3: Speaks understandably, despite noticeable errors. Generally fluent, only occasional miscommunication. Shows good grammatical and vocabulary range. Shows initiative and flexibility.

2: Uneven proficiency: may be strong in one area and weak in another. For example, speech may be fluent but lack range and accuracy; or speech may be accurate but very slow and labored. Understandable with some difficulty, may misunderstand spoken English. Examiner may have to speak slowly and use simple English.

1: Speaks little and with great effort. Difficult to understand. Speaks in short phrases. May be very passive; does not contribute to the conversation. Has difficulty understanding; even simple questions may have to be repeated by the examiner.

Keys, Scripts, and Commentary for Practice Tests

Part 2 Practice Test Keys, Scripts, and Commentary

Key, Script and Commentary for Part 2, Practice Test 1

Do not look at the key and script until you have taken the practice test. Then score your test using the key. Finally, review the practice test by playing the tape recording as you read the script. Do *not* look at the key or script until you have finished the entire test. You will only harm yourself by doing so.

Key to Part 2, Practice Test 1

1. a	11. b	21. c	31. b	41. b
2. a	12. a	22. a	32. a	42. a
3. b	13. b	23. c	33. a	43. a
4. c	14. a	24. a	34. b	44. b
5. a	15. b	25. c	35. c	45. c
6. c	16. c	26. b	36. b	46. b
7. a	17. a	27. c	37. c	47. a
8. a	18. b	28. b	38. b	48. a
9. b	19. a	29. c	39. c	49. c
10. c	20. c	30. c	40. a	50. c

Script and Commentary for Part 2, Practice Test 1

This part contains what is actually recorded on the audio cassette tape that accompanies this book. The tape recording includes all the instructions as well as the cue questions and statements. The tape recording does not include the answer choices. They are printed in the test booklet. The correct answers are marked with an asterisk (*). After each test problem, a short explanation is given.

Part 2, Practice Test 1

This test contains several kinds of problems. There are short questions, for which you should choose the appropriate answer or reply. There are short statements and dialogues, for which you should choose the appropriate paraphrase or summary. There are short statements, in which certain words are emphasized. For these you should choose an appropriate continuation of the statement, that is, what the speaker would say next. Finally, there will be a lecture and longer conversation. During the lecture and conversation, you may take notes on your answer sheet. After the lecture and conversation, you will be asked questions about them.

Here is an example of the short question type of problem. Look at the answer choices printed in your test booklet as you listen:

> Ex. I   When's she going on vacation?
> a. Last week.
> b. To England.
> *c. Tomorrow.

The correct answer is *c, Tomorrow,* because that is the best response to the question. Choice *c* has been marked on your answer sheet to show that it is the correct answer.

Here is an example of the short statement type of problem. You should choose the statement that means about the same thing as what you heard.

> Ex. II   (Male voice): That movie was pretty bad.
> (Female voice): It sure was!
> a. She disagrees that it was good.
> *b. She agrees that it wasn't good.
> c. She agrees that it was beautiful.

The correct answer is *b, She agrees that it wasn't good.* Choice *b* has been marked on your answer sheet for example II.

Here is an example of the emphasis type of problem. You will hear a statement that is spoken in a certain way, with special emphasis. You should listen for the emphasis and interpret it. Choose the answer that tells what the speaker would probably say next.

> Ex. III   I needed the *small* red cup.
> The speaker would continue...
> *a. not the big one.
> b. not the green one.
> c. not the plate.

The correct answer is *a, not the big one,* because the speaker emphasized the word "small." Choice *a* has been marked on your answer sheet for example III.

Now we will begin Practice Test 1. Turn the page to problem 1. For problems 1 through 12, choose the appropriate response to the question.

1. How're they going to get there?
   *a. In Sue's car.
   b. Sue's parents are.
   c. Before noon.

The word *how* is the key to this problem. It asks not who (choice *b*) or when (choice *c*), but how (by what means) they will get there.

2. What would you like to do after dinner tonight?
   *a. See a movie.
   b. I'd like to.
   c. Steak and potatoes.

The speaker asked about what to do. This needs an answer that contains a verb about doing something.

3. Would the train between New York and Chicago be cheaper than the plane?
   a. Yes, I've been there twice.
   *b. No, it's about twice as expensive.
   c. No, it takes twice as long.

"Cheaper than" should let you know prices are being compared.

4. When you were in the teacher's office, what were you talking about?
   a. Not in the office.
   b. At 2 o'clock.
   *c. My last test.

The speaker wanted to know *what* was being talked about.

5. Don't you want to go?
   *a. Yes, I do.
   b. No, she doesn't.
   c. Yes, she will.

"Don't you" may sound like "don'she," but it does require the listener to answer for him/herself, rather than for the "she" in answers *b* and *c*.

6. If you're having trouble with those scissors, why don't you use mine?
   a. Yes, you can use them.
   b. No, you don't.
   *c. Because yours aren't any better.

To answer this, you need to give a reason *why* you won't use the speaker's scissors.

7. I need to meet with you but I work during your office hours. What can I do?
   *a. Make a special appointment with me.
   b. My office is in room 203.
   c. My office hours are from 9 to 11.

The speaker needs to know what to do, not where the office is or when the regular office hours are.

8. Do you want me to stay until you're finished?
   - *a. If you want to.
   - b. No, I'm not.
   - c. Yes, I'm finished.

This kind of question is not really asking for information. It is typical of conversational English. The speaker is trying to be polite. The speaker wants to be told what to do. He knows the person he is talking to is not finished yet. Rather than telling exactly what to do, the answer leaves it up to the speaker.

9. What do you think about going to the movies with our neighbors tonight?
   - a. Late last night.
   - *b. Sounds like fun.
   - c. They'll go with you.

The key here is "what do you think." The speaker is asking for an opinion about her suggestion for something to do.

10. If it hadn't rained all last week, would the river have flooded?
   - a. The river flooded.
   - b. When it rained last night.
   - *c. It might have.

This is grammatically based: it is a negative conditional. We know from what the speaker said that it did rain last week, and the river did flood. The speaker is wondering what would have happened if it did *not* rain last week.

11. I'm going to be working in New York City next year. What's the most common way to get around?
   - a. Near Central Park.
   - *b. The subway.
   - c. Straight down 5th Avenue.

"The most common way to get around" is an idiom, meaning the most usual means of transportation. It doesn't mean where it is or how to get to it.

12. Why didn't you have Fred get the papers?
   - *a. He wasn't here.
   - b. In order to get them.
   - c. For the secretary.

The first part of the question, "Why didn't you," may sound like "Why din't chew," making it more difficult to understand. The question asks for a reason why a person (Fred) didn't do something.

For problems 13 through 28, choose the answer that means about the same thing as the statement or short dialogue you hear.

13. Please give Mary a hand with that work; otherwise she'll never be able to leave on time.
    a. Mary did the work.
    *b. Mary needs help.
    c. Mary left on time.

This is another idiom: to "give someone a hand" means to help them.

14. Joe didn't get here until the meeting had already started.
    *a. He arrived after it started.
    b. He arrived before it started.
    c. He arrived after it ended.

Your knowledge of grammar will help you on this one. Joe didn't arrive until after it had started (he was late). Nothing is said about the meeting being over when he finally arrived.

15. In spite of the fact that Jane disliked big cities, she decided to spend her vacation in London.
    a. Jane didn't go to London.
    *b. Jane will go to London.
    c. Jane likes big cities.

This is a grammar/logic problem. Jane did not like big cities, but she did decide to spend her vacation in London, which is a big city. The contrary connector, "in spite of," should warn you that what you hear in the first part of the sentence will be contradicted in the second part. Getting this problem right depends, to some extent, on the length of your memory span.

16. What with limited funds, and little equipment, it's a wonder we accomplish anything around here.
    a. We don't get anything done.
    b. We need more work to do.
    *c. We get some things done.

This is a complaining remark. The speaker means that despite bad conditions, they still manage to accomplish some things. "It's a wonder," means it's remarkable, or it's unusual.

17. Helen usually gets her father to buy her groceries for her.
    *a. He buys her groceries.
    b. She buys him groceries.
    c. She buys her own groceries.

This is somewhat colloquial. To "get someone to do something" means that you convince them to do it for you.

18. She'll be here any time now.
    a. She's here now.
    *b. She's coming soon.
    c. She comes often.

This is colloquial. "Any time now" or "any day now" means sometime soon.

19. Tom's job had to be finished by his brothers.
    *a. His brothers finished it.
    b. Tom finished it.
    c. They all finished it.

The modal verb "had to" means the brothers were obligated to do it. Tom started the job but did not finish, and the implication is that his brothers finished it alone, without him.

20. John would be better off writing all those figures down first, before he starts trying to add them all up; then he'll have a record to check.
    a. John should add them first.
    b. John should check them first.
    *c. John should make a record first.

The speaker is expressing an opinion on how to do something. To be "better off" means he thinks it is the best way to do it. The speaker lists steps in the process, and says which he thinks should be done first.

21. Arnold wants to reconsider his plans to sell his house.
    a. He won't sell it.
    b. He will sell it.
    *c. He'll think about it.

To "reconsider" means to think again about something. First, he planned to sell his house, but now he wants to think it over.

22. No sooner had Michael gotten off the bus he'd taken to work than he realized he'd left his briefcase behind.
    *a. He had forgotten it.
    b. He left it at work.
    c. He'll get there soon.

He left the briefcase on the bus. You can infer (guess) that he probably forgot it. As soon as he got off the bus, he remembered his briefcase.

23. I heard that the robber escaped from the penitentiary.
    a. He got the money.
    b. He was released from prison.
    *c. He's no longer in prison.

A penitentiary is a jail, or prison. He's no longer there because he escaped, or ran away without permission. Choice *b* is wrong because "released" means to be allowed legally to leave.

24. That man is older than he looks.
    *a. He doesn't look so old.
    b. He is always overlooked.
    c. The man read the books.

This problem tests your understanding of sounds of words. "Looks" might sound like "books," and "older . . . looks" might sound like "overlooks."

25. There are quite a few students taking Dr. Smith's American history class this semester.

   a. Smith's students are quiet.
   b. Smith doesn't have many students.
   *c. Smith has many students.

"Quite a few" means many. Don't confuse quiet and quite!

26. (Female voice): Can you take over for me for a few minutes while I take a short break?
   (Male voice): Sure, no problem.

   a. He can fix the broken equipment.
   *b. He'll replace her for a while.
   c. He'll take it there for her.

In this short dialogue, several colloquialisms are used. "Take over" for her means to replace her, or do her work while she's away. "A short break" means a brief time away from work, to rest. The man is willing to help her out by doing her work while she is away briefly.

27. (Male): What documents do we have to bring to registration?
   (Female): Your identity card or school ID.

   a. He doesn't need to take anything.
   b. She can register him now.
   *c. He should take some identification.

He is planning to register, but won't do it now. She tells him what he needs to take when he registers.

28. (Male): I think I'd better leave. This discussion isn't getting us anywhere.
   (Female): I couldn't agree more.

   a. They think the discussion was useful.
   *b. They're having an argument.
   c. They'll leave together.

This short dialogue has implications, in other words, the two people don't say directly what they mean. Sometimes "discussion" means an argument. They have been discussing something, but can't agree, so the man has decided to leave. The woman agrees that their discussion has failed.

The next problems are of the emphasis type. For problems 29 through 36, choose the answer that is what the speaker would probably say next.

29. I thought you said you were making *chicken* for dinner...

   a. not Dad.
   b. not for lunch.
   *c. not beef.

The kind of food, chicken, is emphasized, so the correct answer would be a contrast, a different kind of food. Beef is the only other kind of food.

30. *Mary* spent the last four months preparing for her exams...
    a. not her camping trip.
    b. not the last two.
    *c. not Elizabeth.

A person's name is emphasized. Choice *a* would contrast with "exams," and choice *b* with "the last four months."

31. I thought your mother was going to be at *home* today...
    a. not tomorrow.
    *b. not at work.
    c. not your father.

The mother's location, a place, is emphasized.

32. I'd like the *red* napkins left out...
    *a. not the green ones.
    b. not the placemats.
    c. not put away.

A color adjective, red, is emphasized.

33. I thought Bonny *visited* London during the month of June...
    *a. not moved there.
    b. not all summer.
    c. not Rome.

A verb telling what she did is emphasized.

34. They are recommending that warnings be posted on all *windows*...
    a. not painted.
    *b. not doors.
    c. not requiring it.

A noun naming a part of a building is emphasized.

35. Bill has lots of *time* to go on vacation...
    a. but not to do his work.
    b. but Joe doesn't have time.
    *c. but not enough money.

An object, not a person, is emphasized.

36. I think Tom should just call the *assistant* bank manager...
    a. not go there.
    *b. not the head manager.
    c. It's Tom's job.

An adjective modifying the manager is emphasized.

Now you will hear a lecture. As you listen, you may take notes about the lecture. Write the notes on your answer sheet. After the lecture is finished, you will be asked some questions about it.

Lecture (about 2 minutes)

Pollution due to overpopulation is a problem in many of the world's developed countries. The northeast corner of the United States is no exception. On the northeast coast of the United States, bordering the Atlantic Ocean, there are many environmental problems related to pollution. There are many causes, but scientists say they are primarily due to land development and its consequence, overpopulation. Some of these pollution problems are quite obvious, while others aren't really noticeable to the general populace. Development has brought changes you can't ignore, like more houses, more boats, and more traffic jams. But there are other changes that you can't see, changes in the marine environment that warn of problems.

At Woods Hole, Massachusetts, researchers at the Woods Hole Oceanographic Institute study the marine fauna—that is, sea animals. The researchers warn that signs of stressed environment are present. When examining a sample of the marine fauna, marine biologists have noticed that now there are fewer species as compared to thirty or forty years ago. In some cases, there is only one single culture of one single species. The existence of only a single species is the big tip-off to stressed environment according to marine biologists. For example, there's the hardshell clam. It can live where other shellfish can't. But the hardshell clams at Woods Hole are so polluted that they can't be used for food, though they can be used as seed clams to populate shellfish beds elsewhere.

In some places the shellfish bed pollution is so bad and consequent bacteria counts have been so high that recreational swimming beaches have to be closed, and people are surprised. But they shouldn't be, because the problem's been creeping up on them a house lot at a time. They've been continuing to develop new housing areas, which demand fresh water and sewerage treatment.

This problem may now be worst in the Northeast area, but is also occurring in other parts of the United States that are experiencing population growth Furthermore, demographers predict that by the turn of the century, 75 percent of the U.S. population will live within fifty miles of an ocean or one of the Great Lakes.

End of the lecture. Now you will be asked seven questions about it, problems 37 through 43. You may use any notes you have taken.

37. What are the *visible* signs of development?
    a. polluted water
    b. fewer shellfish
  *c. traffic jams, more houses and boats
In paragraph 1, these were given as examples of "changes you can't ignore," and they are visible. They are contrasted with "other changes you can't see," choices *a* and *b,* which are talked about later in the lecture.

38. What are the *invisible* warning signs of encroaching pollution?
    a. traffic jams, more houses and boats
  *b. changes in marine fauna
    c. closéd beaches

These are the things not included in the correct answer to problem 37. Choices *a* and *c* are visible signs.

39. What do marine biologists say is the key sign of a "stressed" environment?
    a. Water becomes polluted.
    b. Clams become polluted and can't be eaten.
  *c. The number of marine fauna species is reduced.

In paragraph 2, "fewer species" is given as an example of a sign of a stressed environment. It's an important sign, because the lecturer says it's "the big tip-off." A "tip-off" is a clue to a puzzle or mystery. Choice *a* is the problem, not a sign of it, and choice *b,* the clam, is given as an example.

40. According to the lecture, what is the original source of the pollution?
  *a. land development
    b. high bacteria counts
    c. a stressed environment

In the first paragraph, scientists says the environmental problems are primarily due to land development and overpopulation. Choices *b* and *c* are results, not causes, of pollution.

41. What has happened to the hardshell clam at Woods Hole?
    a. It has died off.
  *b. It is so polluted it can't be eaten.
    c. It can't be used as a seed clam.

At the end of paragraph 2, the lecturer says the clam is "so polluted it can't be used for food." Choices *a* and *c* are not true: in both cases the opposite is true.

42. What happens to make people realize how polluted the marine environment is?
  *a. Beaches are closed to swimmers.
    b. Clams and fish have died off.
    c. The beachfront is crowded with houses and boats.

In paragraph 3, the lecturer says the people are surprised when they find the beaches closed. You can infer they were unaware of the problem until then. Choices *b* and *c* are wrong because the people don't realize the problem even when those things are happening.

43. What does the lecturer predict will happen by the year 2000 for the United States population?
  *a. 75 percent will live within fifty miles of an ocean or the Great Lakes.
    b. 50 percent will live within seventy-five miles of an ocean or the Great Lakes.
    c. Those living in the Northeast will have the greatest problems.

This is a question asking for detail. The answer is in the last paragraph. Choice *b* is wrong because the numbers are reversed, and choice *c* describes the situation now, not in the future.

Now you will hear a conversation between two people. As you listen, you may take notes on your answer sheet. After the conversation, you will be asked some questions about it.

Dialogue (about 4½ minutes)

Male Voice (M): Oh, hi there. You're on the tour, too, aren't you?

Female Voice (F): Oh, yeh, I am. Let's see, you were sitting near the front of the bus, weren't you?

M: Yes, my...

F: And let's see, you're Tim, aren't you?

M: Yeh, my name's Tim Mercer.

F: And I'm Linda Johnson.

M: Well, hi again. Enjoying the free time?

F: Yes, but on the whole, I don't even mind the more "conducted" parts of the tour.

M: Oh?

F: At first, I thought it might be a little *too* well organized, you know, herding us around and stuff...

M: Yeh, me too, but it hasn't been so bad, has it?

F: No, and I appreciate knowing I'll have a place to sleep at night and that my dinner's been paid for in advance.

M: Yeh, that's primarily why we came on this tour. Mother just doesn't want to take chances on not having a place to stay at night scheduled well in advance.

F: So you're traveling with your mother?

M: Yeh, I managed a vacation so I could take one with my mother. She's been a little lonely since Dad died, so I thought we could go off together and get her away from some of those painful memories.

F: Oh, how nice of you. So how do you like *this* quaint little town?

M: It's very pretty. I had a look at the local farm museum. Very interesting.

F: Oh, I haven't been there. What was it like? I went to the gardens, they were beautiful, lots of roses.

M: Hmm...Mother would probably like that—actually she's probably already been there. We split up and I went to the museum.

F: Oh, yes. What was there?

M: Really interesting stuff—old wooden hay rakes and early threshing machines—butter churns—some photo displays of an old flour mill that was near here....

F: That sounds like a good spot to go to. Now, where is that, anyway?

M: Have you got the map they gave us?

F: Yeh, it's right here.

M: Well, let's see...we're at about...oh, right here, number 16 on the map, the circular drive around the monument. Let's see—the museum—it's somewhere on one of the east-west streets—State Street...oh, here it is, number 12 on the map.

F: Oh, good. I'd like to see all those things. Hmm...I wonder if I should go now or wait till after lunch. About how long did it take you to go through it?

M: About an hour, but I tend to get involved in the details of each display, so maybe it wouldn't take someone else so long, maybe only thirty minutes or so. It's pretty small, but it's interesting if you're into that sort of thing.

F: Well, I'm not sure . . . oh, what's that package? Something from the museum?

M: No, they don't sell anything but postcards there. This is an antique teacup and saucer I got for my mother.

F: Oh, that's nice. Where'd you get it?

M: Well, there are several antique shops around . . .

F: Yes, I remember the tour conductor emphasizing that. This is supposed to be an antique-lover's paradise. There are so many antique shops, I don't know where to go first . . .

M: Well, I went into only two of them. They were right next to each other on Kilmer Street.

F: Now where's that?

M: Well, here on the map, you can see it's just south of us. The two shops I saw are numbers 7 and 9 on the map.

F: Oh, I see. Where did you get your teacup?

M: I got it at "The Old Cupboard," that's number 9. The one next to it is "Mercer's Antiques."

F: What were they like?

M: The two shops?

F: Yeh . . .

M: Well, Mercer's had bigger things, like furniture—desks, big tables, cupboards, and so on. But I just wanted something small, some little souvenir.

F: I see. Did you notice if they had any silverware?

M: Hmmm . . . I think both do.

F: I collect silver spoons, and I might like to get another one for my collection.

M: Yeh, I'd try them both if I were you. I think either of those stores would be a little less expensive than the ones closer to the center of town, say on Main Street, and they're a little out of the way, so they wouldn't be so crowded.

F: I think I'll head over there now, before lunch.

M: If you'd like, you're welcome to join Mother and me for lunch. She's going to meet me at a restaurant in about half an hour.

F: Why, how nice of you. Sure, where are you meeting?

M: It's called "The Cheese Board." It's pretty close to here, but so is everything, right? Let's see, it's number 26.

F: Now, where's that . . . oh, here it is, sort of on that funny angle corner . . . Washington and what would that be . . . oh, yes, Washington and State.

M: Yeh, Washington angles down right from where we are now. This restaurant specializes in cheese, of course, and they have sandwiches, and soups, and salads too.

F: That sounds good. Well, I'll head over to look for spoons, and I'll see you and your mother at noon at the Cheese Board.

M: Right. Good luck with the spoon hunting.

End of the conversation. Now you will be asked seven questions about it, problems 44 through 50. You may use any notes you have taken.

44. Why did the man and his mother choose to travel with a tour?
    a. They weren't familiar with the area.
   *b. To be sure of a place to stay at night.
    c. They wanted to save money.

At the beginning of the conversation, the man says his mother wanted a place for the night scheduled in advance.

45. What did the man just buy?
    a. postcards
    b. spoons
   *c. a teacup

He says he bought the teacup for his mother. The woman wants to buy spoons. The farm museum sells postcards, but the man doesn't say he bought any there.

46. Look at the map on your answer sheet. Where did the man make his purchase?
    a. #7
   *b. #9
    c. #12

This is a detail question. The two antique stores he went into were #7 and #9. #9 is "The Old Cupboard." The symbol # means number, so #7 means number 7.

47. Where was the woman earlier this morning?
   *a. the gardens
    b. the museum
    c. the Cheese Board

She says she went to the gardens, and liked the roses. The man went to the museum. The Cheese Board is a restaurant.

48. What were the man and woman afraid might happen during the tour?
   *a. All their activities would be planned for them.
    b. They might not find a place to stay at night.
    c. They might not have money for dinner.

At the beginning of the conversation, the woman says she was afraid it might be too well organized. Choices *b* and *c* are wrong because those were things she was afraid would happen *without* a tour.

49. Look at the map on your answer sheet. What is number 12 on the map?
    a. Mercer's Antiques
    b. the Cheese Board
   *c. the farm museum

This is another detail question. Number 12, the farm museum, is on State Street.

50. What does the man say about Main Street stores?
    a. They have a larger selection.
    b. They're convenient and cheaper.
   *c. They're more crowded and expensive.

He recommends the stores on Kilmer Street to the woman because they're less expensive and crowded than the ones on Main Street.

End Practice Test 1.

Key, Script, and Commentary for Part 2, Practice Test 2

Do not look at the key and script for part 2, Practice Test 2 until you have taken the practice test. Then score your test using the key. Finally, review the practice test by playing the tape recording as you read the script. Do *not* look at the key or script until you have finished the entire test. You will only harm yourself by doing so.

Key to Part 2, Practice Test 2

1. c	11. b	21. b	31. a	41. b
2. b	12. a	22. b	32. c	42. a
3. a	13. c	23. b	33. b	43. c
4. a	14. b	24. c	34. a	44. b
5. c	15. a	25. a	35. c	45. a
6. a	16. c	26. c	36. c	46. c
7. b	17. a	27. b	37. b	47. b
8. c	18. b	28. c	38. a	48. c
9. a	19. c	29. b	39. c	49. c
10. a	20. c	30. b	40. a	50. a

Script and Commentary for Part 2, Practice Test 2

This part contains what is actually recorded on the audio cassette tape that accompanies this book. The instructions consist of what is recorded on the tape. The examples and problems consist of what is recorded as well as the printed answer choices. The correct answers are marked with an asterisk (*). After each test problem, a short explanation is given.

Part 2, Practice Test 2

This test contains several kinds of problems. There are short questions, for which you should choose the appropriate answer or reply. There are short statements and dialogues, for which you should choose the appropriate paraphrase or summary. There are short statements, in which certain words are emphasized. For these you should choose an appropriate continuation of the statement, that is, what the speaker would say next. Finally, there will be a lecture and longer conversation. During the lecture and conversation, you may take notes on your answer sheet. After the lecture and conversation, you will be asked questions about them.

Here is an example of the short question type of problem. Look at the answer choices printed in your test booklet as you listen:

> Ex. I   When's she going on vacation?
>   a. Last week.
>   b. To England.
> *c. Tomorrow.

The correct answer is *c, Tomorrow,* because that is the best response to the question. Choice *c* has been marked on your answer sheet to show that it is the correct answer.

Here is an example of the short statement type of problem. You should choose the statement that means about the same thing as what you heard.

> Ex. II   (Male voice): That movie was pretty bad.
>   (Female voice): It sure was!
>   a. She disagrees that it was good.
>   *b. She agrees that it wasn't good.
>   c. She agrees that it was beautiful.

The correct answer is *b, She agrees that it wasn't good.* Choice *b* has been marked on your answer sheet for example II.

Here is an example of the emphasis type of problem. You will hear a statement that is spoken in a certain way, with special emphasis. You should listen for the emphasis and interpret it. Choose the answer that tells what the speaker would probably say next.

> Ex. III   "I needed the *small* red cup."
>   The speaker would continue . . .
>   *a. not the big one.
>   b. not the green one.
>   c. not the plate.

The correct answer is *a, not the big one,* because the speaker emphasized the word *small.* Choice *a* has been marked on your answer sheet for example III.

Now, we will begin Practice Test 2. Turn the page to problem 1. For problems 1 through 10, choose the appropriate response to the question.

> 1. Where can I find Professor Johnson's office?
>   a. No, I don't think you can.
>   b. If you want to.
>   *c. At the end of the hall.

The speaker asked *where* the office is.

> 2. When Tom comes home, do you think he'll give me a hand with the party decorations?
>   a. Maybe he came to the party.
>   *b. If he's not busy.
>   c. Yes, he gave them to me.

The speaker is asking for an opinion in a hypothetical future situation. This needs a conditional (if) answer.

3. Do you think you'll be able to stop by the cleaners and get my coat on the way home from work tonight?
    *a. Sure, I'll do it.
    b. After I go to the cleaners.
    c. On my way home.

The speaker was asking a favor: please get his coat. "Do you think you'll be able to" means "please."

4. What exactly does she disapprove of about this program?
    *a. It's hard to say.
    b. Yes, she can improve it.
    c. No, I can't prove it.

"Disapprove" may sound like "improve" or "prove." The speaker is asking what is disapproved of. Rather than telling exactly what, the answer shows uncertainty.

5. How do you find life in the city?
    a. I take the bus.
    b. My brother told me how.
    *c. I enjoy it.

"How do you find" in this context means "what is it like" or "what do you think about."

6. Would you mind giving this to the teacher for me tomorrow?
    *a. Sorry, I'm not going to class.
    b. Sorry, I don't mind.
    c. Yes, please give it to her.

The speaker is asking a favor: please give this to the teacher. "Would you mind" is a polite way of asking a favor. The response is a polite refusal to do the favor. It is polite because it gives a good reason for not being able to do the favor.

7. Do you think you can give me more help than you've been giving me lately?
    a. Yes, Mary has.
    *b. No, I can't.
    c. Yes, it was late.

"Lately" means recently. The speaker is asking the listener to help her more.

8. If I'm having trouble, when can I come to your office?
    a. Sure, no problem.
    b. At my office.
    *c. On Friday.

The speaker wants to know *when* he should come to the office for help—if he needs it.

9. You know that secretarial job you have open—how much do you count for typing speed?
    *a. It's quite important.
    b. 50 words per minute.
    c. Open it quickly.

That the job is "open" means that it is available, that they want to hire someone for it. The speaker wants to know how important it is to be a fast typist in order to get the job.

10. Do you think I should finish writing this, or go to the store first?
    *a. Do the writing first.
    b. Both of them will.
    c. OK, I'll go there first.

The speaker asks for an opinion. He wants someone to decide which thing to do first.

For problems 11 through 28, choose the answer that means about the same thing as the statement or short dialogue you hear.

11. The orchestra had been practicing for over six hours when the conductor finally let them go home.
    a. They went home at 6 o'clock.
    *b. They practiced more than 6 hours.
    c. They are still practicing.

"Over" six hours means more than six hours of practice. The conductor let them leave after the practice.

12. John said he'd never had such a good time as he did at the party last Saturday night.
    *a. He liked the party.
    b. He doesn't like parties.
    c. He didn't go to the party.

John is comparing other parties to last night's party. "Never had such a good time" means last night was the best time he'd ever had.

13. They told me something that made me quite upset.
    a. My news pleased them.
    b. My news surprised them.
    *c. Their news bothered me.

They told the speaker and she was "upset," meaning disturbed or bothered.

14. They'd better leave in five minutes or it'll be too late to get to work on time.
    a. It's better if they wait.
    *b. They should go soon.
    c. They were 5 minutes late.

This is a hypothetical or conditional situation. If they don't leave soon (five minutes), then they will be late.

15. Jack could've gone to the Capitol Building while visiting Washington, but he didn't.
    *a. He didn't go to the Capitol Building.
    b. He visited the Capitol Building.
    c. He didn't visit Washington.

Jack was in Washington. He was able to visit the Capitol Building, but he didn't do it.

16. Although we'd never been to Greenville before, we felt right at home there.
    a. We like living there.
    b. We used to live there.
    *c. It was like home to us.
It was their first time in Greenville. Although they had never been there before, they felt comfortable (as if they were "at home") there.

17. Mark should've been wearing a hat.
    *a. He didn't wear one.
    b. He did wear one.
    c. He will wear one.
He should have but he didn't.

18. I'm going on vacation, and I was wondering if you'd mind if I left my car at your house while I'm away.
    a. I want to stay at your house.
    *b. I want you to keep my car.
    c. I went away on vacation.
The speaker will go away in the future. He has not gone yet. He is asking a favor.

19. It wasn't so much his appearance as it was his manner that put me off.
    a. I liked the way he looked.
    b. I didn't like the way he looked.
    *c. I didn't like the way he acted.
The speaker disliked both his appearance (the way he looked) and manner (the way he acted), but disliked his manner more.

20. He must've finished the report.
    a. He should do it.
    b. He needs it.
    *c. He probably did it.
Here, "must have" means "probably" or "certainly" rather than "was obliged to." The speaker thinks he has done the report.

21. John says his new position is working out fine.
    a. John is working outside.
    *b. John likes his job.
    c. John exercises at work.
"New position" means "new job." "Working out fine" means it is going well for him.

22. The workers are supposed to receive a pay raise unless the profits aren't as great as projected.
    a. A raise was given.
    *b. A raise will probably be given.
    c. Large profits aren't expected.
This is a prediction and depends on logic. The profits are expected to be good. If they are good, there will be a pay raise.

23. We shouldn't have let her do it by herself.
    a. We wrote a letter.
    *b. She did it alone.
    c. She was helped.

She did do it by herself. The speaker thinks that was a mistake.

24. Alan filled us in on the details of the development project.
    a. He solved it.
    b. He finished it.
    *c. He explained it.

To "fill someone in on" means to give an explanation or details.

25. (Male voice): Betty didn't leave already, did she?
    (Female voice): I'm afraid she did.
    *a. Betty is gone.
    b. Betty is afraid to leave.
    c. Betty is going to leave.

He asks if Betty left. The woman says Betty did leave. When she says she's "afraid," she means she's sorry Betty left.

26. (Female): Tom, would you be able to help me move these boxes?
    (Male): I'm sorta tied up right now. Why don't you try me again in an hour or so?
    a. He's moving now.
    b. He'll help for an hour.
    *c. He can't help her now.

She asks for help. He says he's "tied up," meaning he's busy now. He'll probably be able to help her after an hour.

27. (Male): Were you able to get any information about Mr. Richards' flight?
    (Female): Not really. All they'd say was that a lot of incoming flights are being rerouted because of the fog.
    a. They got incorrect information.
    *b. They don't know when Richards will arrive.
    c. They know Richards' arrival time.

She was unable to get any detailed information, so they don't know when the flight will arrive.

28. (Female): How long will it take?
    (Male): I would think it could be done in a week.
    a. He can't do it in a week.
    b. He did it a week ago.
    *c. He'll probably need a week.

The work is not done yet, and he estimates that he can do it in a week.

The next problems are of the emphasis type. For problems 29 through 37, choose the answer that tells what the speaker would probably say next.

29. Peter's driving to New York tomorrow...
    a. not flying.
    *b. not Chicago.
    c. not today.

The name of the city (New York) is emphasized, in contrast to another city (Chicago). Neither the method of travel (driving as contrasted to flying) nor the time (tomorrow rather than today) is emphasized.

30. Excuse me, but I asked for one large scoop of chocolate ice cream...
    a. not two.
    *b. not a small one.
    c. not vanilla.

The size of the scoop (spoonful) is emphasized, so an adjective indicating size is needed.

31. The dean wants the graduates to be known for their *technical* skills...
    *a. not their writing skills.
    b. not the teachers.
    c. not the university.

The kind of skills is emphasized, so another kind of skills is the right answer.

32. If Bob broke the T.V., he should replace it...
    a. not the radio.
    b. not just repair it.
    *c. not you.

A pronoun is emphasized, so the answer will be another pronoun or a person's name.

33. No, I said the coat was too small for Henry...
    a. not too large.
    *b. not for Robert.
    c. not the sweater.

The name of the person who doesn't fit the coat is emphasized, so another person is the right answer.

34. She always borrows my car...
    *a. not sometimes.
    b. not Harry's.
    c. not my bicycle.

An adverb describing the frequency (how often) of the thing happening is emphasized, so another adverb of frequency is needed.

35. No, it wasn't Ellen who told Dan...
    a. Ellen wrote him.
    b. Ellen told Martha.
    *c. Martha told him.

The name of the person who did not tell him is emphasized, so the answer will be the name of the person who did tell him.

36. But I wanted to walk <u>through</u> the park...
    a. not to ride.
    b. not the zoo.
    *c. not around it.
The way (or route) the person wanted to walk in relation to the park is emphasized.

37. I only <u>suggested</u> that you type the report again...
    a. not the letter.
    *b. not demanded.
    c. not write it.
A past-tense verb is emphasized, so another past-tense verb will be the correct answer.

Now you will hear a lecture. As you listen, you may take notes about the lecture. Write the notes on your answer sheet. After the lecture is finished, you will be asked some questions about it.

Lecture (about 1½ minutes)

Albert Richards is now a retired dental professor from the University of Michigan. Twenty-five years ago, he was teaching radiography (that's X-ray techniques) to U of M Dental students. As he walked past a five and dime store one day, he noticed daffodils on sale for only 25 cents a dozen. He bought that bargain bunch of flowers and took it back to his lab, where it became a bargain bigger than he had imagined.

He began using radiography not just on teeth and skeletal bones, but on flowers. Over the years, he's perfected his method of X-ray photography, and now has assembled a collection of over 2800 images of flowers (that is, X-ray radiographs). Everyday photographic film records reflected or transmitted visible light; but X-ray image results from variations in the thickness & composition of the subject. Richards' flowers look like ghostly, three dimensional gray glass models of flowers. They appear transparent, because of X-ray's unique ability to penetrate. Furthermore, X-rays yield black & white images, a medium of expression many find more challenging than color photography. Richards passes X-rays through his subject onto a piece of 5 by 7 X-ray film, which he then uses as a negative to make his prints.

Much of his time is spent in preparation, finding the right bloom, carefully grooming and arranging it, and then waiting for it to turn to just the right alignment to suit his composition.

End of the lecture. Now you will be asked six questions about it, problems 38 through 43. You may use any notes you have taken.

38. What was Richards' original bargain, according to the lecture?
    *a. a bunch of daffodils
    b. radiographs of flowers
    c. a visit to a five and dime store
In the first paragraph, the lecturer says Richards bought a bunch of daffodils for the bargain (low) price of 25 cents a dozen.

39. What is radiography?
    a. black and white photography
    b. a purely dental technique
    *c. X-ray photography
The lecturer says Richards was teaching radiography, or X-ray techniques, to dental students.

40. How are Richards' photographs different from normal, usual ones?
    *a. They are recorded on X-ray film.
    b. They are in black and white.
    c. They reflect light onto radiographs.
The flowers are photographed using X-ray photography, or radiography, rather than "everyday photographic film." All the X-rays photos are in black and white, but ordinary photographs may also be in black and white.

41. What does normal, everyday photographic film do?
    a. yield black and white images
    *b. record reflected transmitted light
    c. penetrate X-rays
In the second paragraph, the lecturer says normal photographs record "reflected or transmitted visible light."

42. How does radiography differ from normal photography?
    *a. X-rays penetrate the subject.
    b. X-rays reflect transmitted light.
    c. X-rays don't require light.
While normal photographs "record reflected light," X-rays pass through the object being photographed. In the second paragraph the lecturer says X-rays have a "unique ability to penetrate" and that "Richards passes X-rays through his subject."

43. What do Richards' flowers look like, as compared to normally photographed flowers?
    a. They reflect light.
    b. They are black and white.
    *c. They are transparent.
In the second paragraph, the lecturer says "They appear transparent." Normal photographs use reflected light, and could be either color or black and white.

Now you will hear a telephone conversation between two people. As you listen to the conversation, you may take notes on your answer sheet. After the conversation, you will be asked some questions about it.

Dialogue (about 4 minutes)

Female Voice (F): Hello, Bridgetown Library.

Male Voice (M): Hi, Bridgetown Library?

F: Yes, can I help you?

M: Yeh, I just moved to the area and I'm trying to find out about the library. First, how do I get books out?

F: Well, first you'd need a library card. You can come in and show us your driver's license, and we can issue a card right away.

M: OK, so first I get my card. What's the limit on books? Five or six?

F: No, there's no limit for adults on the number of books you can check out, but they can be kept for only two weeks.

M: Very good. How about your hours? I'm especially interested in weekends, since I work during the week.

F: Well, we're a very small local library, so we have rather restricted hours. We're open Monday through Thursday noon to five, and all day Friday—we open at nine then, and Saturdays from nine to noon.

M: OK, so that's weekday afternoons, and Saturday mornings . . . that leaves me out on weekdays, but Saturdays—Saturdays are OK. Too bad you're not open Sundays.

F: Well, as I said, we're pretty small.

M: Do you have anything special for kids? I've got two little preschoolers . . . they're still pretty young, and don't read yet.

F: Well, we do have an extensive juvenile section for young readers, but you might be interested in our Story Time for very young children. It's on Friday mornings. The story time is advertised in the *Town Crier.*

M: The time sounds OK. My wife can probably bring the kids. But what's the *Town Crier?*

F: Oh, that's a local newspaper. You can get it at various stores in the area, like the IGA.

M: The IGA?

F: Yes, that's the I-G-A food market in Bridgetown. We're located just across the street from it.

M: Well, how *do* I get there?

F: Have you got a map?

M: Yeh, I think I've got one somewhere—OK, yeh, here it is.

F: Now where are you located?

M: We live just south of Portage Lake, right off Mount Hope Road.

F: OK, so you've got to get from Mount Hope over to us. The town's between Center and Territorial Roads, and pretty much bounded by Glenn to the north and Water Street to the south. Now you could just go up Mount Hope and then take Territorial around, but that's rather circular.

M: Yeh, it does look that way. How about cutting across? I could take Hoffman off Mount Hope and go east . . . Now my map doesn't have all the road names marked . . .

F: OK, so you're going east on Hoffman off Mount Hope . . . Don't go all the way up to Miller Road—that crosses Hoffman later—when you come to a fork, Hoffman is the left-hand fork going north, and you'll continue east on—let me think—yes, it's Ballou Road.

M: OK, Ballou Road east at the fork, then that runs into Territorial, doesn't it?

F: Yes, that's right. When you get to Territorial, turn left—that's north and continue right into the town of Bridgetown.

M: OK, now where exactly are you located?

F: OK, the first street past Water Street has a yellow blinking light. Turn right there . . .

M: OK, I'll mark that "number 1" on my map. None of these little streets are labeled.

F: Then go two blocks to the IGA . . .

M: OK, I'll mark that "number 2."

F: And we're just across the street, on the left-hand side.

M: Oh, yes, I think I know now where that is. I'll mark that "3" on my map. Well, thank you very much. You've been very helpful. You'll probably be seeing a lot of us.

F: Oh good, I hope so. Thanks for calling. Bye!

M: Goodbye.

End of the conversation. Now you will be asked seven questions about it, problems 44 through 50. You may use any notes you have taken.

44. What is the limit on the number of books that can be checked out?
    a. No limit, but they must be returned in six weeks.
    *b. No limit, but they must be returned in two weeks.
    c. Six books every two weeks.

At the beginning of the conversation, the man asks if there is a book limit. The librarian tells him there's no book limit for adults, but they can be kept for only two weeks.

45. What times would be especially good for the man to visit the library?
    *a. Saturday mornings
    b. Friday evenings
    c. weekday afternoons

The man says he works during the week, and the library isn't open Friday evenings.

46. Look at the map on your answer sheet. What is the name of the road connecting Hoffman and Territorial Roads?
    a. East Fork
    b. Miller Road
    *c. Ballou Road

This is one of the unmarked roads on the man's map. Ballou Road is the name of the right-hand fork. It goes east, but it isn't named East Fork.

47. When is the story time for young children?
    a. Saturday mornings
    *b. Friday mornings
    c. weekday afternoons

The librarian tells the man this in the middle of the conversation. He thinks his wife can take their children then.

48. How can someone find out about the story times?
    a. A notice is mailed to parents.
    b. They're posted in the IGA food market.
    *c. They're advertised in the *Town Crier*.

This is in the middle of the conversation. The *Town Crier* is a local newspaper.

49. Look at the map on your answer sheet. When the man gets to the fork in Hoffman Road, what should he do?
    a. go straight
    b. go north
    *c. go east

He should take Ballou Road, the right fork. He will then be traveling east. The north fork is a continuation of Hoffman Road. He cannot go straight.

50. Again, look at the map. What is located at number 1?
    *a. a blinking light
    b. the food market
    c. the library

The man marked this on his map. It's at the first street past Water Street. The food market is at number 2, and the library at number 3.

End Practice Test 2.

Part 3 Practice Test Keys and Commentary

Key to and Commentary on Part 3, Practice Test 1

Key to Part 3, Practice Test 1

Grammar

1. a	7. a	13. b	19. d	25. a
2. a	8. d	14. a	20. a	26. a
3. d	9. b	15. c	21. c	27. b
4. b	10. c	16. d	22. d	28. c
5. d	11. c	17. b	23. b	29. b
6. c	12. c	18. a	24. d	30. a

Cloze

31. c	35. a	39. d	43. b	47. d
32. d	36. c	40. a	44. a	48. c
33. b	37. c	41. a	45. c	49. b
34. a	38. c	42. a	46. d	50. a

Vocabulary

51. a	57. a	63. b	69. d	75. c
52. c	58. c	64. b	70. d	76. b
53. b	59. b	65. d	71. d	77. d
54. a	60. d	66. b	72. b	78. a
55. d	61. c	67. b	73. a	79. c
56. a	62. a	68. a	74. a	80. b

Reading

81. b	85. b	89. b	93. c	97. c
82. d	86. d	90. b	94. b	98. c
83. a	87. c	91. b	95. d	99. a
84. a	88. a	92. d	96. a	100. b

Commentary on Part 3, Practice Test 1

Grammar

1. a. "Majority," like "most" or "a lot of," quantifies "scientists," and "scientists" takes the plural verb form.

2. a. In the subject position, a gerund form ("locking") is needed at the head of the clause.

3. d. Tests choice of modal verb as well as tense. Since the choice of asking for a ride was an option in the past, a past tense form of the modal verb should be used.

4. b. Tests relative clause. Can be correct with or without "which," but relative clauses never take an additional pronoun ("it" or "them"). "Afraid of" is an adjective plus a preposition and the preposition "of" can't be deleted.

5. d. The noun "failure" is modified by the adjective "constant." "Because of" needs to be followed by a noun phrase, i.e., a noun ("failure") plus pronoun ("his") plus adjective ("constant").

6. c. "Are" requires a verb ("interested"). "Have" would require a noun such as "interest." "Interesting" is wrong because it is an adjective describing what the students are like rather than how they feel about art.

7. a. This is a hypothetical question (here an offer of possible help), so the "if" is needed. "What" is needed since it is a question. "As if" would be used for comparison.

8. d. The verb "seem" needs the infinitive "to be."

9. b. This is an embedded relative clause. "What" is needed because it means "the thing that."

10. c. Tests passive voice and the adverb form "easily."

11. c. The connector "although" should not have another connector at the beginning of the second clause, just subject plus verb clause.

12. c. Tests choice of preposition for use with the verb "trust." Sometimes verbs often used with certain prepositions are called "two-word" verbs. It is best to memorize them as a unit.

13. b. Tests choice of modal; "must" means the speaker is certain.

14. a. "That" refers to the problem; "other than" means everything else about the cake, like "except for" or "besides." The wrong answers b and c are nonsensical.

15. c. The verb "impressed" requires the preposition "by" or "with" in this context.

16. d. The present progressive tense is needed here. The infinitive "to guard" would also be acceptable.

17. b. The gerund "doing" is used with the two-word verb "thought of" here. A gerund or noun phrase is needed after a preposition (of).

18. a. In this clause, "how" is used alone to modify "expensive."

19. d. This tests verb choice ("have" or "do") and past perfect tense. "Wish" plus the reference to the past make the past perfect tense necessary.

20. a. Pronouns ("it," "them") are not used at the end of relative clauses; this sentence uses active rather than passive voice.

21. c. Infinitive followed by gerund is correct here; "finish" takes the gerund.

22. d. This gerund uses the passive voice. Either a noun phrase (such as "new employment") or a gerund ("being hired") must be used here, following the "of."

23. b. The adjective "quite" modifies "enough," which in turn modifies "hot." "Too" cannot modify "enough."

24. d. The pronoun "them" referring to carrots is used as the object. It cannot be deleted.

25. a. A comparative, "than," should be used rather than a preposition.

26. a. The word order must take the question form, and the modal "have to" requires the auxiliary verb "do."

27. b. The infinitive of an active verb is used here. Many adjectives (such as "easy," "difficult," "nice," etc.) are commonly followed by infinitives.

28. c. This adjective string tests word order used with "so." "Such a lovely" would also be acceptable.

29. b. "Moreover" is the only connector to express addition; all the other connectors given would be used for a second phrase with a contrary or contrasting meaning.

30. a. This adverb is a negative quantifier and should be memorized much as vocabulary is.

Cloze

31. c. A singular noun meaning study or investigation is needed here.

32. d. A plural noun that refers to the source of the data or evidence is needed here.

33. b. An adjective modifying a plural noun is necessary.

34. a. The clause connector "that" is necessary.

35. a. A noun is needed; we know from the first sentence that this passage will concern shifts in climate.

36. c. A noun meaning a set space of time, "period" fits here.

37. c. A plural noun meaning climate or weather itself is needed here. Changes or shifts in weather do not fit.

38. c. A quantifiable noun is required. Weather, sun, and crop cannot rise and fall.

39. d. To fit here, the verb must mean the opposite of "falls." "Ups" and "high" are not verbs, and "increase" is grammatically incorrect.

40. a. The past tense of "take" is needed here. "Was" cannot be used with place, and "in" is not a verb.

41. a. The pronoun "they," which follows in the sentence, indicates that both England and Europe are being referred to.

42. a. "Than" is needed to express the contrast or change in the weather pattern.

43. b. All the other choices would make this an incomplete or run-on sentence.

44. a. A comparative adjective is needed here; "warmer" would be contradictory to the sense of the sentence.
45. c. A noun meaning an area or location is needed here.
46. d. A verb expressing belief or thought is needed here.
47. d. A noun meaning change or alteration is needed here.
48. c. This adjective locates the part of the atmosphere where the change occurred. A descriptive adjective such as "windy" does not make sense in this context.
49. b. "By" is the only preposition that goes with the two-word verb "governed by."
50. a. A verb expressing a change is needed here. "Turn" is semantically incorrect in this context.

Vocabulary

51. a. Here, positive, meaning "certain," or "sure," can be contrasted with "uncertain" or "unsure"; positive is also the opposite of negative.
52. c. Somewhat colloquial. To "trail" someone is to follow after him, in his path or trail.
53. b. Informal but common term; can also be used to mean to get someone's attention.
54. a. An involuntary shaking or shivering; can be caused by excitement, fear, cold, etc.
55. d. A meeting that is unplanned or brief.
56. a. To confuse or perplex. As a noun, can mean a barrier or partition.
57. a. To be unhappy from loss of hope or confidence.
58. c. A colloquialism, meaning as fast and as easy as to "snap one's fingers." A "snap" is a sharp, cracking sound.
59. b. Can also mean ineffective; not strong. A very old or very sick person may be "feeble," as may a poor response or argument.
60. d. Can also mean reliable; related to the noun "creed," a formal statement of beliefs.
61. c. To think carefully about something.
62. a. An informal term meaning to push roughly.
63. b. To be reluctant, and usually complaining; semantically related to the verb "begrudge."
64. b. "Common" in the sense of being widespread or predominant.
65. d. Often used in the sense of taking risks or chances, as "speculators" in the stock market.
66. b. To be "ignorant of" means not to know about.
67. b. This means strong. "Muscular" would be used only for living organisms and is not appropriate for an inanimate object.
68. a. The same semantic meaning as a method. The other choices, while semantically related, are inappropriate here.
69. d. A colloquialism meaning to be able to interpret beyond what was actually written *on* the lines, thus to "see *between* the lines" of writing.
70. d. To speak very quietly and indistinctly. The wrong answer choices are unrelated to speaking.

71. d.   A boundary or wall; "frontier" would be used for a geographical marker.
72. b.   This means being healthy, growing well, and is often used in referring to crops.
73. a.   To scatter lightly with water or rain.
74. a.   Completely and without reservation or conditions.
75. c.   To keep over a period of time.
76. b.   Characteristics of a person or thing. "Principles" would be related to moral virtues, "functions" to uses.
77. d.   To handle awkwardly and with difficulty. Sometimes people "fumble for words" when they don't know what to say.
78. a.   To be slow and uncertain about a decision.
79. c.   To draw the opponent's attention away; related to "diverge," meaning to go in different directions.
80. b.   Needing great energy or exertion. "Ardent" would be used to express strong feelings.

Reading

81. b.   The second paragraph explains that pharmacologists and cell biologists are interested in sponges because of their chemical compounds, which may be used in drugs in the future.
82. d.   In the first paragraph, the author says "they have been around for centuries," in other words, they have survived despite their primitive form.
83. a.   In the second sentence, the author says sponges are primitive, then gives examples to justify this: lack of muscles and nerves, no mouth or digestive cavity, no organs.
84. a.   In paragraph two, "after centuries in the bathtub" means sponges have been used for bathing, as well as for general cleaning.
85. b.   The first sentence states that until the 19th century, sponges "were called zoophytes, the animal-plants."
86. d.   The passage states that "for a baby with impaired hearing, the peaks *take* longer [not *are* longer] to appear," and that in "conductive deafness, which can be treated, wave patterns will emerge [appear or show themselves] if the intensity of the sound is increased." Choice *a* would be true of untreatable deafness and choice *c* is true for normal infants.
87. c.   The electrodes "pick up," or detect, "the electrode activity thus evoked [stimulated] in the brain."
88. a.   "Absence of all...waves indicates total sensory-neural deafness, usually untreatable." Also see item 86.
89. b.   After amplification, the electrical signals are "fed into a computer and printed out...."
90. b.   The first sentence stresses the importance of early detection of deafness. No mention is made in the passage of accuracy or learning to administer or interpret the test.
91. b.   The first paragraph tells of how 19th-century magicians used scientific inventions to produce "magic." The second paragraph uses the magician Etienne Robert to exemplify this.

92. d. The first paragraph tells that magicians used traditional skills in combination with new scientific inventions. Choices *a* and *b* would be examples of traditional skills; choice *c* can be ruled out because nowhere does the passage say the magicians were more intelligent than the public.

93. c. Near the end of the passage, it is stated that the images were projected onto the smoke, and that the movements of the smoke made them appear to be alive.

94. b. The passage states that "images were projected from [Robert's] concealed magic laterns."

95. d. The entire second paragraph can be seen as an example of what is stated more generally in the first paragraph. See also item 91.

96. a. The passage states that the mushrooms become "soggy," or filled with moisture, if steady heat is not maintained.

97. c. In the second sentence, the author states that "freezing produces erratic [unpredictable] results," and that it depends on the species.

98. c. The brick cap is a kind of mushroom. In the third sentence, the author states that the brick cap fruits late in the fall; it is given as an example of a species that freezes well.

99. a. Here, the storage technique used (jars) is the only procedure given that will protect properly prepared mushrooms. The other choices all concern preparation of mushrooms.

100. b. At the beginning of the second paragraph, the author states that "good circulation of warm air...is the most important principle." "Steady heat" is also stressed, but does not appear as an answer choice.

Key to Part 3, Practice Test 2

Grammar

1. a	7. a	13. b	19. a	25. a
2. c	8. b	14. a	20. c	26. d
3. d	9. d	15. a	21. a	27. b
4. d	10. c	16. d	22. d	28. c
5. b	11. a	17. b	23. b	29. d
6. a	12. c	18. c	24. a	30. d

Cloze

31. d	35. c	39. d	43. b	47. d
32. b	36. a	40. a	44. c	48. a
33. a	37. c	41. d	45. b	49. b
34. c	38. d	42. a	46. b	50. d

Vocabulary

51. d	57. b	63. a	69. c	75. b
52. c	58. d	64. b	70. a	76. c
53. a	59. b	65. a	71. b	77. d
54. b	60. a	66. a	72. c	78. b
55. d	61. a	67. d	73. c	79. b
56. c	62. c	68. d	74. a	80. d

Reading

81. c	85. d	89. b	93. d	97. d
82. c	86. d	90. b	94. a	98. a
83. a	87. d	91. d	95. a	99. a
84. a	88. a	92. c	96. b	100. c

Commentary on Part 3, Practice Test 2

Grammar

1. a. The gerund form, "going," is needed as the object of the preposition.

2. c. This tests word order in a subordinate phrase. "So" intensifies the adverb "often" which modifies the verb "happens." Each modifier should occur just before the word it modifies. "Too" cannot be used here because it is part of a subordinate phrase.

3. d. The appropriate verb tense in this context is future perfect. "By noon" lets you know it is not noon yet; later, when it is noon, the speaker will be finished.

4. d. The correct connector should express a contrary thought; all the incorrect answers express addition.

5. b. The existential "there" is necessary here.

6. a. This is a standard comparative phrase, "as . . . as." "So . . . as" could also be used since the sentence is negative.

7. a. The passive form of the verb is needed here, since the action will be done to the clothing, not by the clothing.

8. b. This is a noun compound, testing the form of the adjectives modifying the noun "period." A preposition should not be included, and any plural markers would be on the noun, not the adjectives.

9. d. Often, the present progressive is used in a future context. "Will be held" would also be correct. Here the verb requires the passive voice, because the convention cannot perform the action.

10. c. The correct preposition, "between," expresses the relationship between two people.

11. a. Here the preposition is part of a two-word verb. "Called off" means canceled. The other prepositions used with "call" have different meanings.

12. c. This tests word order in reported speech. "It was shipped" is a subordinate phrase.

13. b.   "Another" can be used only for a singular noun; "other" is an adjective modifying the noun "skills" and does not need a plural marker.

14. a.   This is the past tense of a passive verb.

15. a.   "Which" must be included in this relative clause. "That" could also be used here.

16. d.   This is the active form of the verb; "be baked" would be the correct passive form.

17. b.   This tests word form ("nothing") plus a negative connector. A comparison ("nothing than") is inappropriate here.

18. c.   This tests present perfect verb tense. The action (to know) is completed and continual.

19. a.   This tests the correct adjective form for the stem "suit." "Suiting" and "suited" are verbs, while "suitably" is an adverb.

20. c.   Here two infinitives are used together. The meaning is that he had to stop (in order) to make the call, not to stop the action of calling.

21. a.   An embedded verb (let + pronoun + do), rather than an infinitive (let + pronoun + to do) is needed here, and the relative pronoun ("it") is necessary.

22. d.   This tests word order in a clause; placing the preposition at the end is informal but acceptable.

23. b.   The present perfect is the only acceptable tense here, since the action (forgetting) is completed, and the speaker specifies the present time (now).

24. a.   This is a relatively formal conditional (hypothetical) statement, using inverted word order. "If we had known," using normal word order, would also be correct.

25. a.   The gerund ("drinking") is the object of the sentence, and expresses a continual daily action, which the speaker wishes to stop. Choices c and d are the wrong tense, and "to drink" would mean that every day the person must stop for a drink of coffee.

26. d.   This calls for choice of the correct relative pronoun. "What" is an emphatic type of expression here. Choices a and b would appear in a subordinate clause, and "how" is not a pronoun.

27. b.   A verb ("doing") and gerund ("building," meaning the action of building) appear in an embedded clause. Choices c and d use an incorrect tense, and a does not use a gerund form.

28. c.   "Mostly" is a positive quantifier of the adjective "black." It means most of the pencils are black.

29. d.   For this conditional ("even if"), "if" is necessary to show the action might happen in the future.

30. d.   In questions, normal word order is inverted, so here the auxiliary verb "can" must appear first; "done" is the correct passive form of the verb.

Cloze

31. d.   To fit here, the noun must mean the opposite of "benefit."

32. b.   A modal expressing necessity fits here.

33. a.   A coordinating conjunction (connector expressing addition) is needed here.

34. c.   This is the only preposition that expresses the correct meaning. "And" is not a preposition.

35. c.   A connector expressing a resultant action is needed here. Choices *a* and *b* do not fit grammatically, and choice *d* is contradictory and illogical.

36. a.   This is the only appropriate preposition. Choice *d* is not a preposition.

37. c.   To fit here, the noun must express a thought or worry. The other choices are semantically incorrect.

38. d.   A connector ("so") is needed here to express resultant action.

39. d.   An adjective meaning ideal, optimum, or proper is needed here.

40. a.   An article is needed here, and would precede any adjective string.

41. d.   A negative quantifier is needed here.

42. a.   To be semantically correct, the noun chosen must express a problem or difficulty. It refers to the "concern" in item 37.

43. b.   The noun here must express a period of time. Choice *a* would refer to a series of actions rather than a period of time.

44. c.   The incorrect answers do not fit semantically and do not make sense.

45. b.   The noun here must express the researchers' final objective.

46. b.   This is the only appropriate preposition.

47. d.   The verb with auxiliary is needed here; the structure is parallel ("goal is to find . . . and to be able").

48. a.   The degree complement here ("so . . . that") should express causality.

49. b.   An infinitive is needed here. It could also take the form "in order to."

50. d.   An adjective expressing the opposite of "optimal" is needed here, to contrast "positive" with "negative."

Vocabulary

51. d.   Something that is meaningful or notable. Like a *sign, sign*ificance can show something.

52. c.   Used figuratively for persons to indicate anger; related to fumes or smoke from a fire. Choice *d* is absurd and would mean the person himself was burning or smoking.

53. a.   This means long and careful thought. Juries in courts of law are said to "deliberate" while reaching a decision.

54. b.   This is colloquial, referring to a person's intentions or purpose.

55. d.   This means to ask for, or look after someone else's concerns.

56. c.   This means strange or unusual, away from the center or norm, literally "off center."

57. b.   This has negative connotations, to be unpleasantly surprised.

58. d.   A loud, unruly disturbance.

59. b.   To go along with as a guide, to accompany. One person can "escort" another.

60. a.   Often used in a judicial setting, when a defendant states that he was somewhere else when a crime was committed.

61. a.   Also means friendly, easy to get along with.

62. c.   The "fore" is the front, or beginning; a leader is at the front of his field. Here, Tom is the leader who is the "most" in "front."

63. a. To assert is to claim the truth of one's statement.

64. b. Also, to put together.

65. a. Well-known in the sense of being highly regarded.

66. a. This means compacted, or pushed together. Choice c means to make stronger, so does not fit this context.

67. d. A place where fruit trees grow. "Cultivation" refers to the process of caring for crops, and "harvest" to the gathering of crops.

68. d. Something, usually a disease, that is transmitted involuntarily, or "caught." Sometimes laughter is said to be contagious. "Congenial" means friendly, "accessible" means obtainable, and "compulsory" means required.

69. c. This means to weaken and grow smaller due to lack of water.

70. a. This means the rest of it, what was left. Choices c and d would refer to small pieces or fragments.

71. b. This means visually unclear. Choice a cannot refer to a printed object, and choice c would be used with reference to a feeling of dizziness.

72. c. This refers to his feelings about the idea. If he is "resigned to" the idea, he has accepted it, though he is not happy about it. "Destined" has to do with fate; "indulged" is incorrect because while one can indulge oneself and one's desires, one cannot indulge an idea.

73. c. This means a bright light.

74. a. This means having a second choice or option, something different.

75. b. This means rough and uneven, not smooth.

76. c. Something that cannot succeed is "futile."

77. d. While choices b, c, and d all mean a final result, choice d is further used more specifically, to mean an opinion that is formed or a decision that has been made.

78. b. This means at the same time.

79. b. This means to accept others' opinions or practices.

80. d. This means soon, within a few moments. Choices a and b would refer to something of great importance, and choice c means with attention to small details.

Reading

81. c. The canals are an example of a disastrous remedy; they were constructed for drainage which was supposed to "increase food production."

82. c. The passage states "the canals became arms [extensions] of the sea and salt water intruded [entered]" into the croplands.

83. a. The last sentence states that "increasing salinity [salt water]...threatens the nursery...of the...shrimp"; therefore too much salt in the water is bad for them (this makes choice b incorrect). They need some fresh water mixed in, so choice a is correct. Nothing is said about moving water (choice c) or the temperature of the water (choice d) as far as the shrimp are concerned.

84. a. The salt water intrudes "in periods of drought" (when there is lack of rain).

85. d. The passage states people thought the muck "was going to waste" (not being used), and they wanted to use it.

86. d. At the beginning of the passage, it is stated that consumption of bakery products is increasing, and further, that baked goods as a source of carbohydrates are replacing rice and other grains. While carbohydrates (cereals) are advocated as good protein carriers, the passage states that little has so far been done in this area. (Also see question 87.)

87. d. The last sentence states "carbohydrates . . . are logical protein carriers."

88. a. The second sentence of the second paragraph states that they are now being phased out (their use is being slowly reduced and stopped).

89. b. The second and third sentences give this information, that there is a preference for compounded bakery products, and Japan is an example of countries following this trend.

90. b. The second half of the second paragraph gives this information. India is given as an example of a country where consumption of protein-enriched bread is encouraged, and the last sentence states that cereals are logical protein carriers. (Also see question 87.)

91. d. The third sentence states the thesis, and the second paragraph gives examples of how this is achieved.

92. c. The passage states that "fat is accumulated . . . to store the energy necessary for lactation."

93. d. The second sentence of the second paragraph states that "nutrients [are] transported via the uterine and placental blood systems," and the following sentence refers to these blood systems as a "lifeline."

94. a. The passage states that "preparation for lactation . . . will take place even at the expense of fetal growth." This means that the mother's body "thinks" lactation is more important than the baby.

95. a. The question asks what was, but is no longer believed; the second sentence of the passage states the belief.

96. b. The passage states that there was "no competent [able] architect in the colonies."

97. d. Shadwell is referred to as Thomas Jefferson's "paternal home," meaning it belonged to his father, Peter.

98. a. The passage states Monticello "was developed in intermittent stages as its busy master [Thomas Jefferson] found opportunity." This means Jefferson would work at it a while, then stop, then work some more.

99. a. The last sentence states that Jefferson "was the first exponent in America" of the classical revival style. An "exponent" tries to promote something.

100. c. The passage states that the house was begun in 1769 and not finished till after 1809; Jefferson moved into the house in 1770, after Shadwell "had been destroyed by fire."

Scoring and
Interpreting Your Test

Scoring and Interpreting Your Test

When you take the official MELAB, all your test papers will be sent to the English Language Institute of the University of Michigan (ELI-UM) for grading. Approximately two to three weeks later, the ELI-UM will send you an official score report. The score report will tell you your final score (the average of your scores on parts 1, 2, and 3) and your separate part scores. If an oral interview was given, ratings will have been reported to ELI-UM by the local examiner, and those ratings will be given on the score report form. Oral interview ratings are on a different scale from the one used for the other parts of the test and are not averaged in with the final score. The ELI-UM will report your score to you and to any institutions (schools or universities) to whom you have asked your scores to be sent.

The scores reported are *not* the total number of problems answered correctly, nor are they percentage scores. Rather, they are scaled scores. The scaled scores are based on statistical average, or "normal" scores from past test administrations. The average score for each part (parts 1, 2, and 3) is approximately 73–75. Here are possible score ranges and average scores for each part.

Possible Score Range	Chance (Guessing)	Average (Mean)	Part of MELAB test
99–33	45	74	Final (Avg. of parts 1, 2, 3)
97–53	—	73	Part 1 (Composition)
100–30	45	75	Part 2 (Listening)
100–15	40	73	Part 3 (Gr., Cl., Voc., Read.)
4$^+$–1	—	2$^+$	Oral Interview

The practice tests in this book are not the same as the official MELAB, but they can give you a general idea of how you would perform on the official test. The problems in the practice test were written by actual MELAB test writers and experimentally pretested, but were not used on actual MELAB tests.

For part 1, the composition, you cannot really score your test yourself. You should practice writing and ask your teacher to review and criticize your work. Your teacher may use the composition descriptions and sample essays as a guide, but you and your teacher should know that only evaluators trained at the ELI-UM are qualified to grade MELAB essays.

For part 2 (Listening) and part 3 (Grammar, Cloze, Vocabulary, Reading), count the number of correct answers. Here is an approximation of your equated, or scaled, score on each of these two parts. Different forms of the MELAB subtests are not of the same difficulty level. The "equated" scores are meant to produce equivalent scores from tests of unequal difficulty. Therefore, "raw" scores (the number correct) needed to achieve a certain "equated" score will vary (be different depending on the form of the test).

Part 2 No. Correct (Range)	Part 3 No. Correct (Range)	Equated, or Scaled Score Range (Estimated)	English Proficiency Level Description
47–50	90–100	95–100	Comparable to edu-
43–47	79–89	90–94	cated native speak-ers of English
37–42	68–82	85–89	Advanced
30–38	60–72	80–84	
25–34	53–64	75–79	Adv. Intermediate
23–28	45–56	70–74	Intermediate
20–24	38–51	65–69	Low Intermediate
18–21	35–45	60–64	Adv. Elementary
15–18	31–37	55–59	
13–16	29–33	50–54	
12–13	26–31	45–49	
10–12	25–27	40–44	
5–9	20–24	35–39	Elementary
1–6	15–19	30–34	
0	10–14	25–29	
0	5–9	20–24	
0	0–4	15–19	

For example, suppose you answered 23 problems correctly on Listening Practice Test 1. You can see on the part 2 range that your score of 23 could fall into the 23–28 category *or* the 20–24 category and would "equate" to either the 70–74 or the 65–69 scaled score range. Since your score of 23 is near the top of the 20–24 category, and at the bottom of the 23–28 category, you can estimate that the scaled score would be close to 69 or 70.

The ELI-UM does not make recommendations for admission based on MELAB scores. Each institution (university, college, business, or profession) sets its own standards for admission based not only on English test scores but on other factors as well. These other factors could be scores on other tests, such as the SAT, GRE, GMAT, or LSAT, or the Cambridge Syndicate or other British English and scholastic exams (O levels, A levels). The institutions also consider previous academic record and grade point average as very important. Letters of recommendation from your professors or work superiors are also considered.

Generally, the ELI-UM recommends that the institution consider your level of study (undergraduate or graduate) and your field of study. Students at the undergraduate level might need greater English language proficiency than those at the graduate level, who will be studying a field that they already know. Students studying in the social sciences and humanities fields will probably need greater English language proficiency than those studying technical fields, such as math or engineering. Students thinking of qualifying for a Ph.D. will need greater reading and writing skills.

Different institutions (universities) have different score requirements for admission. Some programs at some schools require a score as high as 90; many institutions require a score of 85, or 80 minimum, and some institutions require 75 or as low as 70. Usually the score requirement will depend on whether or not the institution has supplemental English courses available to its students and what program the student wishes to enter.

Some institutions that have English as a Second Language (ESL) programs will admit you to study in their ESL program before beginning studies in your academic field. At other institutions, you may study ESL part-time while studying part-time in your academic field.

Appendixes

Appendix A: MELAB Part 1 (Composition) Form

MICHIGAN ENGLISH LANGUAGE ASSESSMENT BATTERY
PART 1: COMPOSITION

NAME (PRINT) _____ Date _____
             (family/last/surname)   (given/first name)

SIGNATURE _____

INSTRUCTIONS:

1. You will have **30 minutes** to write on <u>one</u> of the two topics printed below. If you do not write on one of these topics, your paper will not be scored. If you do not understand the topics, ask the examiner to explain or to translate them.

2. You may make an outline if you wish, but your outline will not count toward your score.

3. Write about 1 to 2 pages. Your composition will be marked down if it is extremely short. Write on both sides of the paper. Ask the examiner for more paper if you need it.

4. You will not be graded on the appearance of your paper, but your handwriting must be readable. You may change or correct your writing, but you should not copy the whole composition over.

5. Your essay will be judged on clarity and overall effectiveness, as well as on
    - topic development
    - organization
    - range, accuracy, and appropriateness of grammar and vocabulary

---

TOPICS: SET --   (CIRCLE THE LETTER OF THE TOPIC YOU CHOOSE)

  A:

  B:

START HERE:

CONTINUE ON BACK

Appendix B: Official MELAB Composition Descriptions and Codes

MELAB Composition Global Proficiency Descriptions

97. Topic is richly and fully developed. Flexible use of a wide range of syntactic (sentence level) structures, and accurate morphological (word forms) control. There is a wide range of appropriately used vocabulary. Organization is appropriate and effective, and there is excellent control of connection. Spelling and punctuation appear error-free.

93. Topic is fully and complexly developed. Flexible use of a wide range of syntactic structures. Morphological control is nearly always accurate. Vocabulary is broad and appropriately used. Organization is well controlled and appropriate to the material, and the writing is well connected. Spelling and punctuation errors are not distracting.

87. Topic is well developed, with acknowledgment of its complexity. Varied syntactic structures are used with some flexibility, and there is good morphological control. Vocabulary is broad and usually used appropriately. Organization is controlled and generally appropriate to the material, and there are few problems with connection. Spelling and punctuation errors are not distracting.

83. Topic is generally clearly and completely developed, with at least some acknowledgment of its complexity. Both simple and complex syntactic structures are generally adequately used; there is adequate morphological control. Vocabulary use shows some flexibility, and is usually appropriate. Organization is controlled and shows some appropriateness to the material, and connection is usually adequate. Spelling and punctuation errors are sometimes distracting.

77. Topic is developed clearly but not completely and without acknowledging its complexity. Both simple and complex syntactic structures are present; in some "77" essays these are cautiously and accurately used while in others there is more fluency and less accuracy. Morphological control is inconsistent. Vocabulary is adequate, but may sometimes be inappropriately used. Organization is generally controlled, while connection is sometimes absent or unsuccessful. Spelling and punctuation errors are sometimes distracting.

73. Topic development is present, although limited by incompleteness, lack of clarity, or lack of focus. The topic may be treated as though it has only one dimension, or only one point of view is possible. In some "73" essays both simple and complex syntactic structures are present, but with many errors; others have accurate syntax but are very restricted in the range of language attempted. Morphological control is inconsistent. Vocabulary is sometimes inadequate and sometimes inappropriately used. Organization is partially controlled, while connection is often absent or unsuccessful. Spelling and punctuation errors are sometimes distracting.

67. Topic development is present but restricted, and often incomplete or unclear. Simple syntactic structures dominate, with many errors; complex syntactic structures, if present, are not controlled. Lacks morphological control. Narrow and simple vocabulary usually approximates meaning but is often inappropriately used. Organization, when apparent, is poorly controlled, and little or no connection is apparent. Spelling and punctuation errors are often distracting.

63. Contains little sign of topic development. Simple syntactic structures are present, but with many errors; lacks morphological control. Narrow and simple vocabulary inhibits communication. There is little or no organization, and no connection apparent. Spelling and punctuation errors often cause serious interference.

57. Often extremely short; contains only fragmentary communication about the topic. There is little syntactic or morphological control. Vocabulary is highly restricted and inaccurately used. No organization or connection is apparent. Spelling is often indecipherable and punctuation is missing or appears random.

53. Extremely short, usually about 40 words or less. Communicates nothing, and is often copied directly from the prompt. There is little sign of syntactic or morphological control. Vocabulary is extremely restricted and repetitively used. There is no apparent organization or connection. Spelling is often indecipherable and punctuation is missing or appears random.

N.O.T. N.O.T. (Not On Topic) indicates a composition *written on a topic completely different from any of those assigned;* it does not indicate that a writer has merely digressed from or misinterpreted a topic. N.O.T. compositions often appear prepared and memorized. They are not assigned scores or codes.

Code Interpretation

Note: The codes are meant to indicate that a certain feature is *especially good or bad in comparison to the overall level of the writing.*

    a   topic especially poorly or incompletely developed
    b   topic especially well developed

c organization especially inappropriate to material
d organization especially uncontrolled
e organization especially well controlled

f connection especially poor
g connection especially smooth

h syntactic (sentence-level) structures especially simple
i syntactic structures especially complex
j syntactic structures especially uncontrolled
k syntactic structures especially controlled

l especially poor morphological (word forms) control
m especially good morphological control

n vocabulary especially narrow
o vocabulary especially broad
p vocabulary use especially inappropriate
q vocabulary use especially appropriate
r spelling especially inaccurate
s punctuation especially inaccurate

t paragraph divisions missing or apparently random
u handwriting illegible or nearly illegible
v question misinterpreted or not addressed
w reduced one score level for unusual shortness

x other (write-in: see score report)

Appendix C: Official MELAB Score Report and Score Interpretations

ENGLISH LANGUAGE INSTITUTE
TESTING AND CERTIFICATION DIVISION
THE UNIVERSITY OF MICHIGAN
ANN ARBOR, MICHIGAN 48109-1057 U.S.A.

TELEPHONE: (313) 764-2416
763-3452

FAX: (313) 763-0369
TELEX: 4320815

MICHIGAN ENGLISH LANGUAGE ASSESSMENT BATTERY

Candidate's Name:

•

Telephone Number:

ID No.:
Date Arranged:
Date Scores Sent:
Date Tested:
Test Location:
Date of Birth:
Native Language:
Native Country:

Reported to:

Part 1:
COMPOSITION
Topic Score Code(s)

Part 2:
LISTENING TEST
Form   Score

Part 3:
GCVR TEST
Form   Score

OPTIONAL
ORAL RATING

FINAL MELAB
SCORE

COMMENTS:

SUBTEST AND SCORE DESCRIPTIONS

Part 1:
COMPOSITION

A 30 minute impromptu composition, written on an assigned topic. Judged by at least two raters on clarity and overall effectiveness, as well as on topic development, organization and range, accuracy, and appropriacy of grammar and vocabulary. The rating scale has 10 levels: 97, 93, 87, 83, 77, 73, 67, 63, 57, 53. The assigned score is an average of the ratings. Mean (average) score is 73. For complete score descriptions and coded comments, see accompanying description/coding sheet.

Part 2:
LISTENING
TEST

A 30 minute, 50 item tape recorded objective test measuring comprehension of spoken English. Contains single sentence questions and statements, a longer dialogue and lecture on which examinee may take notes. Score range is 100-30. Chance (guessing) score is 45. Mean score is 75.

Part 3:
GCVR
TEST

A 100 item multiple choice test containing grammar, cloze reading, vocabulary problems, and short prose selections followed by comprehension questions. Score range is 100-15. Chance (guessing) score is 40. Mean score is 73.

ORAL
RATING
(optional)

Oral rating supplied by local examiner from 10-15 minute oral interview. Examiner considers communicative effectiveness with regard to overall fluency, range, accuracy, as well as grammar, vocabulary, pronunciation, understanding. Score range is 4+ − 1, with 4 being advanced and 1 being elementary proficiency. Mean rating is 2+. Reliability not established. Not included in Final Score.

FINAL
MELAB
SCORE

The Final Michigan English Language Assessment Battery (MELAB) Score consists of the average of the three parts: Composition, Listening, Grammar/Cloze/Vocabulary/Reading Tests. The oral rating is reported separately. Score range for the Final MELAB Score is 99-33. Chance score is about 45. Mean Final Score is about 74.

NOTE THAT MELAB SCORES REFLECT ENGLISH PROFICIENCY, AND DO NOT NECESSARILY PREDICT ACADEMIC SUCCESS, WHICH IS DETERMINED BY MANY ADDITIONAL FACTORS. See reverse for score interpretation.

MICHIGAN ENGLISH LANGUAGE ASSESSMENT BATTERY
SCORE INTERPRETATION

MELAB FINAL SCORE RANGE	ENGLISH PROFICIENCY LEVEL DESCRIPTION
100-90	Comparable to native speakers of English
89-80	Advanced level English proficiency
79-75	Advanced intermediate level English proficiency
74-70	Intermediate level English proficiency
69-65	Low intermediate level English proficiency
64-60	Advanced elementary level English proficiency
59-below	Elementary level English proficiency

Decisions regarding admission to a program should not be based solely on MELAB scores. NOTE THAT MELAB SCORES REFLECT ENGLISH LANGUAGE PROFICIENCY, AND DO NOT NECESSARILY PREDICT ACADEMIC SUCCESS, WHICH IS DETERMINED BY MANY ADDITIONAL FACTORS. Decisions should be made in accordance with the student's field and level of study, academic background and preparation, local standards, and other data deemed relevant.

The linguistic demands of the student's field of study along with the student's experience and expertise in the field are particularly relevant when using MELAB scores as evidence of sufficient English proficiency for academic study. More advanced level English proficiency may be required for general undergraduate study than for some graduate or professional programs. Graduate students in some technical or performance programs may be able to use their prior knowledge of the subject matter to compensate for deficiencies in general English.

When interpreting MELAB scores, both part scores and the final score should be noted. For example, two students (A and B) have the same final scores but quite different part scores.

	Part 1 Composition	Part 2 Listening	Part 3 GCVR	Final MELAB Score
Student A	65	86	73	75
Student B	77	62	85	75

Even though these individuals have the same final MELAB score, their performance on the three parts suggests differences in their language proficiency. Such differences may be predictive of their facility to use English effectively in different contexts.

If a student is admitted for a reduced academic load plus supplemental English, it is recommended that his academic courses be ones which do not make heavy language demands, such as laboratory or mathematics courses. Correlations of English tests with GPA's (grade point averages) of specialized laboratory courses may be as low as .10, while the correlations may be as high as .40 to .60 for other types of courses with less restricted language.

Due to errors of measurement, an individual's true score may vary from his obtained score. It is estimated that on the MELAB, an individual's true score may be 3 points higher or lower than the score actually obtained. Thus the true score of a student who obtained 77 on the MELAB might be as high as 80 or as low as 74.

Appendix D: Suggested Texts Available from the University of Michigan Press

For Listening and Speaking

Folse, Keith, and Darren Bologna. *Targeting Listening and Speaking: Strategies and Activities for ESL/EFL Students*

Morley, Joan. *Improving Aural Comprehension*

Morley, Joan. *Improving Spoken English: An Intensive Personalized Program in Perception, Pronunciation, Practice in Context*

Morley, Joan. *Listening Dictation*

For Grammar, Vocabulary, Reading

Folse, Keith S. *Intermediate Reading Practices: Building Reading and Vocabulary Skills, 3rd edition*

Reinhart, Susan M. *Testing Your Grammar, Revised Edition*

Silberstein, Sandra, Barbara K. Dobson, and Mark A. Clarke. *Reader's Choice, 4th edition*

Appendix E: Answer Sheets for Practice Sets

MICHIGAN ENGLISH LANGUAGE ASSESSMENT BATTERY
PART 2: LISTENING TEST ANSWER SHEET   PRACTICE TEST 1

Name_____ Native Language _____ Date _____

Ex.I a( )	12. a( )	26. a( )	37. a( )	LECTURE NOTES
b( )	b( )	b( )	b( )	
c(X)	c( )	c( )	c( )	
Ex.II a( )	13. a( )	27. a( )	38. a( )	
b(X)	b( )	b( )	b( )	
c( )	c( )	c( )	c( )	
Ex.IIIa(X)	14. a( )	28. a( )	39. a( )	
b( )	b( )	b( )	b( )	
c( )	c( )	c( )	c( )	

1. a( )   15. a( )   29. a( )   40. a( )
    b( )   b( )   b( )   b( )
    c( )   c( )   c( )   c( )

2. a( )   16. a( )   30. a( )   41. a( )
    b( )   b( )   b( )   b( )
    c( )   c( )   c( )   c( )

3. a( )   17. a( )   31. a( )   42. a( )
    b( )   b( )   b( )   b( )
    c( )   c( )   c( )   c( )

4. a( )   18. a( )   32. a( )   43. a( )
    b( )   b( )   b( )   b( )
    c( )   c( )   c( )   c( )

5. a( )   19. a( )   33. a( )   44. a( )
    b( )   b( )   b( )   b( )
    c( )   c( )   c( )   c( )

6. a( )   20. a( )   34. a( )   45. a( )
    b( )   b( )   b( )   b( )
    c( )   c( )   c( )   c( )

7. a( )   21. a( )   35. a( )   46. a( )
    b( )   b( )   b( )   b( )
    c( )   c( )   c( )   c( )

8. a( )   22. a( )   36. a( )   47. a( )
    b( )   b( )   b( )   b( )
    c( )   c( )   c( )   c( )

9. a( )   23. a( )   48. a( )
    b( )   b( )   b( )
    c( )   c( )   c( )

10. a( )   24. a( )   49. a( )
    b( )   b( )   b( )
    c( )   c( )   c( )

11. a( )   25. a( )   50. a( )
    b( )   b( )   b( )
    c( )   c( )   c( )

CONVERSATION NOTES

MICHIGAN ENGLISH LANGUAGE ASSESSMENT BATTERY
PART 2: LISTENING TEST ANSWER SHEET   PRACTICE TEST 2

Name_____ Native Language _____ Date _____

Ex.I a( )	12. a( )	26. a( )	38. a( )	LECTURE NOTES
b( )	b( )	b( )	b( )	
c(X)	c( )	c( )	c( )	
Ex.II a( )	13. a( )	27. a( )	39. a( )	
b(X)	b( )	b( )	b( )	
c( )	c( )	c( )	c( )	
Ex.IIIa(X)	14. a( )	28. a( )	40. a( )	
b( )	b( )	b( )	b( )	
c( )	c( )	c( )	c( )	
1. a( )	15. a( )	29. a( )	41. a( )	
b( )	b( )	b( )	b( )	
c( )	c( )	c( )	c( )	
2. a( )	16. a( )	30. a( )	42. a( )	
b( )	b( )	b( )	b( )	
c( )	c( )	c( )	c( )	
3. a( )	17. a( )	31. a( )	43. a( )	
b( )	b( )	b( )	b( )	
c( )	c( )	c( )	c( )	
4. a( )	18. a( )	32. a( )	44. a( )	CONVERSATION NOTES
b( )	b( )	b( )	b( )	
c( )	c( )	c( )	c( )	
5. a( )	19. a( )	33. a( )	45. a( )	
b( )	b( )	b( )	b( )	
c( )	c( )	c( )	c( )	
6. a( )	20. a( )	34. a( )	46. a( )	
b( )	b( )	b( )	b( )	
c( )	c( )	c( )	c( )	
7. a( )	21. a( )	35. a( )	47. a( )	
b( )	b( )	b( )	b( )	
c( )	c( )	c( )	c( )	
8. a( )	22. a( )	36. a( )	48. a( )	
b( )	b( )	b( )	b( )	
c( )	c( )	c( )	c( )	
9. a( )	23. a( )	37. a( )	49. a( )	
b( )	b( )	b( )	b( )	
c( )	c( )	c( )	c( )	
10. a( )	24. a( )		50. a( )	
b( )	b( )		b( )	
c( )	c( )		c( )	
11. a( )	25. a( )			
b( )	b( )			
c( )	c( )			

Michigan English Language Assessment Battery
Part 3: Answer Sheet

Form [ ]

ne _____ Native Language _____ Date _____
(Family)   (First)

Grammar

1. a( ) b( ) c( ) d( )
2. a( ) b( ) c( ) d( )
3. a( ) b( ) c( ) d( )
4. a( ) b( ) c( ) d( )
5. a( ) b( ) c( ) d( )
6. a( ) b( ) c( ) d( )
7. a( ) b( ) c( ) d( )
8. a( ) b( ) c( ) d( )
9. a( ) b( ) c( ) d( )
10. a( ) b( ) c( ) d( )
11. a( ) b( ) c( ) d( )
12. a( ) b( ) c( ) d( )

13. a( ) b( ) c( ) d( )
14. a( ) b( ) c( ) d( )
15. a( ) b( ) c( ) d( )
16. a( ) b( ) c( ) d( )
17. a( ) b( ) c( ) d( )
18. a( ) b( ) c( ) d( )
19. a( ) b( ) c( ) d( )
20. a( ) b( ) c( ) d( )
21. a( ) b( ) c( ) d( )
22. a( ) b( ) c( ) d( )
23. a( ) b( ) c( ) d( )
24. a( ) b( ) c( ) d( )
25. a( ) b( ) c( ) d( )

26. a( ) b( ) c( ) d( )
27. a( ) b( ) c( ) d( )
28. a( ) b( ) c( ) d( )
29. a( ) b( ) c( ) d( )
30. a( ) b( ) c( ) d( )

Cloze

31. a( ) b( ) c( ) d( )
32. a( ) b( ) c( ) d( )
33. a( ) b( ) c( ) d( )
34. a( ) b( ) c( ) d( )
35. a( ) b( ) c( ) d( )
36. a( ) b( ) c( ) d( )
37. a( ) b( ) c( ) d( )
38. a( ) b( ) c( ) d( )

39. a( ) b( ) c( ) d( )
40. a( ) b( ) c( ) d( )
41. a( ) b( ) c( ) d( )
42. a( ) b( ) c( ) d( )
43. a( ) b( ) c( ) d( )
44. a( ) b( ) c( ) d( )
45. a( ) b( ) c( ) d( )
46. a( ) b( ) c( ) d( )
47. a( ) b( ) c( ) d( )
48. a( ) b( ) c( ) d( )
49. a( ) b( ) c( ) d( )
50. a( ) b( ) c( ) d( )

Vocabulary

51. a( ) b( ) c( ) d( )
52. a( ) b( ) c( ) d( )
53. a( ) b( ) c( ) d( )
54. a( ) b( ) c( ) d( )
55. a( ) b( ) c( ) d( )
56. a( ) b( ) c( ) d( )
57. a( ) b( ) c( ) d( )
58. a( ) b( ) c( ) d( )
59. a( ) b( ) c( ) d( )
60. a( ) b( ) c( ) d( )
61. a( ) b( ) c( ) d( )
62. a( ) b( ) c( ) d( )
63. a( ) b( ) c( ) d( )

64. a( ) b( ) c( ) d( )
65. a( ) b( ) c( ) d( )
66. a( ) b( ) c( ) d( )
67. a( ) b( ) c( ) d( )
68. a( ) b( ) c( ) d( )
69. a( ) b( ) c( ) d( )
70. a( ) b( ) c( ) d( )
71. a( ) b( ) c( ) d( )
72. a( ) b( ) c( ) d( )
73. a( ) b( ) c( ) d( )
74. a( ) b( ) c( ) d( )
75. a( ) b( ) c( ) d( )
76. a( ) b( ) c( ) d( )

77. a( ) b( ) c( ) d( )
78. a( ) b( ) c( ) d( )
79. a( ) b( ) c( ) d( )
80. a( ) b( ) c( ) d( )

Reading

81. a( ) b( ) c( ) d( )
82. a( ) b( ) c( ) d( )
83. a( ) b( ) c( ) d( )
84. a( ) b( ) c( ) d( )
85. a( ) b( ) c( ) d( )
86. a( ) b( ) c( ) d( )
87. a( ) b( ) c( ) d( )
88. a( ) b( ) c( ) d( )
89. a( ) b( ) c( ) d( )

90. a( ) b( ) c( ) d( )
91. a( ) b( ) c( ) d( )
92. a( ) b( ) c( ) d( )
93. a( ) b( ) c( ) d( )
94. a( ) b( ) c( ) d( )
95. a( ) b( ) c( ) d( )
96. a( ) b( ) c( ) d( )
97. a( ) b( ) c( ) d( )
98. a( ) b( ) c( ) d( )
99. a( ) b( ) c( ) d( )
100. a( ) b( ) c( ) d( )

A Student's Guide to the MELAB